A Voice for Maria Favela

Radical Politics and Education

Series editors:
Derek R. Ford and Tyson E. Lewis

With movements against oppression and exploitation heightening across the globe, radical activists and researchers are increasingly turning to educational theory to understand the pedagogical aspects of struggle. The Radical Politics and Education series opens a space at this critical juncture, one that pushes past standard expositions of critical education and critical pedagogy. Recognizing the need to push political and educational formulations into new theoretical and practical terrains, the series is an opportunity for activists, political thinkers, and educational philosophers to cross disciplinary divides and meet in common. This kind of dialogue is crucially needed as political struggles are increasingly concerned with questions of how to educate themselves and others, and as educational philosophy attempts to redefine itself beyond academic norms and disciplinary values. This series serves to facilitate new conversations at and beyond these borders.

Advisory Board:
Jodi Dean *(Hobart and William Smith Colleges, USA)*
Margret Grebowicz *(University of Silesia, Poland)*
Davide Panagia *(University of California, Los Angeles, USA)*
Patti Lather *(Ohio State University, USA)*
Nathan Snaza *(University of Richmond, USA)*
Stefano Harney *(Singapore Management University, Singapore)*

Also available in the series:
Against Sex Education: Pedagogy, Sex Work, and State Violence, Caitlin Howlett
A History of Education for the Many: From Colonization and Slavery to the Decline of US Imperialism, Curry Malott
Experiments in Decolonizing the University: Towards an Ecology of Study, Hans Schildermans
Rethinking Philosophy for Children: Agamben and Education as Pure Means, Tyson E. Lewis and Igor Jasinski
Althusser and Education: Reassessing Critical Education, David I. Backer

Forthcoming in the series:
Rancière and Emancipatory Art Pedagogies: The Politics of Childhood Art,
Hayon Park
Queers Teach This!: Queer and Trans Pleasures, Politics, and Pedagogues,
Adam J. Greteman

A Voice for Maria Favela

An Adventure in Creative Literacy

Antonio Leal
(Translated by Alexis Gibbs and Diana Sousa)

BLOOMSBURY ACADEMIC
LONDON • NEW YORK • OXFORD • NEW DELHI • SYDNEY

BLOOMSBURY ACADEMIC
Bloomsbury Publishing Plc
50 Bedford Square, London, WC1B 3DP, UK
1385 Broadway, New York, NY 10018, USA
29 Earlsfort Terrace, Dublin 2, Ireland

BLOOMSBURY, BLOOMSBURY ACADEMIC and the Diana logo are trademarks of
Bloomsbury Publishing Plc

First published in 1983 in Brazil as Fala Maria Favela by Editora Ática
First published in Great Britain 2023
This paperback edition published 2024

Copyright © Antonio Leal 1983
English language translation © Alexis Gibbs and Diana Sousa 2023

Antonio Leal, Alexis Gibbs and Diana Sousa have asserted their right under the Copyright,
Designs and Patents Act, 1988, to be identified as Author of this work.

Series design by Adriana Brioso
Cover image © bortonia/iStock

This work is published open access subject to a Creative Commons
Attribution-NonCommercial-NoDerivatives 4.0 International licence
(CC BY-NC-ND 4.0, https://creativecommons.org/licenses/by-nc-nd/4.0/). You may re-use,
distribute, and reproduce this work in any medium for non-commercial purposes,
provided you give attribution to the copyright holder and the publisher
and provide a link to the Creative Commons licence.

Bloomsbury Publishing Plc does not have any control over, or responsibility for,
any third-party websites referred to or in this book. All internet addresses given
in this book were correct at the time of going to press. The author and publisher
regret any inconvenience caused if addresses have changed or sites have
ceased to exist, but can accept no responsibility for any such changes.

A catalogue record for this book is available from the British Library.

A catalog record for this book is available from the Library of Congress

ISBN:	HB:	978-1-3502-4757-4
	PB:	978-1-3502-4761-1
	ePDF:	978-1-3502-4758-1
	eBook:	978-1-3502-4759-8

Series: Radical Politics and Education

Typeset by Integra Software Services Pvt. Ltd.

To find out more about our authors and books visit www.bloomsbury.com
and sign up for our newsletters.

Contents

Foreword	viii
Author's preface to the English edition	xii
Translator's introduction	xiv
Introduction	1
March of '81	4
Play	9
Games	10
Methods	12
Family	18
Special education	24
The student	32
Teaching	42
Community	43
Civics ('Civismo')	57
Cliché	58
Murals	59
A civic episode…	60
The housemaid	62
Illness/hunger/madness	74
Violence	76
Politics	80
Index	95

Foreword

By Inny Accioly

The Rocinha Favela Speaks

Antonio Leal's narrative takes the reader through the history of the Rocinha favela, located in Rio de Janeiro (Brazil) and considered one of the largest slums in Latin America, with more than 48,000 inhabitants currently living there.[1] The author's educational experiences in the early 1980s are intertwined with a valuable historical account of a complex territory that represents the synthesis of the city internationally known as the 'wonderful city', Rio de Janeiro, a city famous for its samba, bossa nova songs and its natural beauty.

It was in Rocinha, in the mid-1990s, during a field trip conducted by my elementary school geography teacher, that I first learned the meaning of the word 'inequality'. At the time, I was a child around eleven years old and lived in a middle-class neighbourhood. *Inequality*: the trip to Rocinha had stamped this word into my dictionary, as painful as it was troubling.

The hill upon which the favela's narrow and overpopulated alleyways have gradually expanded, where the sewers run open and cardboard shacks are piled up next to unpainted and unventilated masonry homes, has a breathtaking view of the São Conrado neighbourhood. This is the favela's 'rich neighbor,' home to the haute bourgeoisie, known for its ostentatious houses and the private security fences that impose the boundaries between the rich and the rest. Rocinha doesn't just speak of inequality; it *screams*. Along with 'resistance' and 'struggle', it is a word that is integral both to the history of Brazil and to the origin of Rocinha.

When investigating the favela's history, Silva (2010) presents versions that relate its growth to the migratory wave of workers from the northeastern region of Brazil, expelled from their lands by the expansion of capitalist agriculture. Historians have also frequently linked the growth of the favelas in Rio de Janeiro to the consequences of the War between Brazil and Paraguay (1865–70). In the

---

[1] Data Rio. Data from 2019. Retrieved from https://www.data.rio/pages/rio-em-sntese-2

confrontation, Black slaves were called to defend the interests of the Brazilian elite in exchange for promises of liberation and rewards that never became a reality.

> (…) We have an interesting question for reflection: as has been said, most of the combatants in the War were black. It leads us to believe that there was a significant impact on the city's socioeconomic structure due to the formal transformation of many slaves into 'free' people. However, the latter did not have an urban territorial space to inhabit; they lived with extreme legal limitations of their possessions. Without the promised wages, subsistence guarantees could only arise from the ability to invent a possible city (…).
>
> (Silva, 2010: 58)

The construction of these 'possible cities' – in this case, the Rocinha Favela – meant a procedural and complex phenomenon, a continuous result of daily struggles to survive and to appropriate a space coveted by the elites, a space of natural beauty, overlooking the sea and relatively close to Downtown.

Silva (2010) questions the discourses about the favelas' origins that erase the memory of the struggles historically undertaken by Black people in Brazil, both in the fight for rights and in the production of knowledge in the fields of art, education, geography, architecture and others. As he states, 'telling the story of the struggle teaches how to struggle' (Silva, 2010).

The lyrics of the song 'favela', by Arlindo Cruz, capture the sociability built into these daily struggles for survival:

O povo que sobe a ladeira	This hillside-dwelling people
Ajuda a fazer mutirão	Is all about the joint effort
Divide a sobra da feira	Whether sharing the market's leftovers
E reparte o pão	Or their daily bread
Como é que essa gente tão boa	How is it that such good people
É vista como marginal	Are seen as delinquents
Eu acho que a sociedade	I think society
Tá enxergando mal	Sees things in the wrong way

Here we find the kinds of community ties which, for instance, are about offering collective support to a neighbour who is building an extension to his home so as to accommodate new family members, or about food sharing among community members, or about providing a support network of care for the children while the mother goes to work as a cleaning lady, as a maid or in another service industry that, in general, reflects the segregation suffered by those that live in the favela.

As stated by Antonio Leal in this work, the story of Maria Favela (a character invented by him and the children throughout the educational process) is a living story. She is a housemaid with a child that she provides for by herself, and whose paternity she does not know. 'This story rings true because it reflects the stories of so many of my students, whose mothers are maids and whose fathers work in factories' (Leal, 2022, p.89).

A remarkable characteristic of the Brazilian elite is to have maids and nannies to whom they delegate the care of their children. It is the concrete expression of a highly racist society in which the elite does not give up their slaveholding traditions. The situation faced by Antonio Leal's students in the early 1980s is, still today, the situation experienced by many women in the favelas: they spend the day taking care of their boss's children, while their own children are left alone at home, under the care of older siblings or women in their neighbourhood. Only in exceptional situations do employers allow their housekeepers to take their children to the workplace, where, from an early age, they suffer the symbolic violence of being children whose lives are treated as less valuable than the lives of the employer's children. An example of this situation occurred in 2020 when the world was facing the pandemic of Covid-19 and schools were closed. Miguel Otávio, a Black kid aged 5, and the son of a housemaid, fell from the ninth floor of a high-class building, his mother's workplace. The fall happened while his mother needed to go outside to walk the family's pet dog, and the boy was under the 'care' of the employer.

In Brazil, the death of Black children does not cause a national commotion. On the contrary, the hegemonic media portrays children from the favelas as criminals, which causes public opinion to accept extremely violent police operations that often result in massacres. The favelas become actual scenarios of war, where disputes between drug trafficking gangs and confrontations with the police establish a daily routine of violence and fear.

Silva (2010) describes aspects of his childhood in the Rocinha favela during the 1980s:

> My childhood was very good and very bad. I played a lot in the alleys and alleyways of the favela, but I also witnessed moments of great violence and loss. One of the most terrible things was the famous 'plastic lifting'. Let me explain. When a person was murdered, the body would be exposed in the street until the hearse arrived. It became an event. Almost every day, you would hear: 'do you know who died?' Some children played a fundamental role in these 'events'. Since, generally, the policemen would 'guard' the deceased, the residents would

stand around waiting for someone (a bold one) to lift the plastic so that one could see the state of the corpse and the way the death had occurred. I was one of the children who usually lifted the plastic.

(Silva, 2010: 19)

Violence and fear often invade the daily life of the favela school and subject teachers and students to a high degree of unpredictability, with frequent disruptions to school routine caused by shootings in the community. In this way, favela children learn from a very young age to 'read' the complex context in which they live.

In the favela, we are told (as 'ordinary' residents) that we need to adopt a type of behavior and attitudes to survive in the place, from the examples we have with the demonstration of strength and the observations of what happens to those who don't follow such 'principles' (…). We build analytical skills to know what to talk about, when to talk, with whom to talk, and, fundamentally, to 'read' (from the most tender age, even if we are not yet literate by school) the contexts of the alleyways. When we get off the bus, for example, at the entrance to the favela, we learn to 'interpret' the favela climate. We read when it's dangerous or calm to go up the hill. Learning to read the context for many children in the favela means surviving.

(Silva, 2010: 19)

It is in this context that Antonio Leal develops the work presented here, sharing with the reader his anguishes, difficulties, and pedagogical strategies, not with the intention of offering a ready-made method to be replicated, but with a disposition towards open dialogue, to learning, and for the collective construction of a transformative education. In this sense, this work is an excellent source of inspiration for critical educators working in the global peripheries.

Inny Accioly
Fluminense Federal University
Rio de Janeiro – Brazil

Reference

Silva, R. T. (2010). Escola-Favela e Favela-Escola: 'Esse menino não tem jeito!'. Tese de Doutorado. Niterói: Programa de Pós-Graduação em Educação, Universidade Federal Fluminense.

Author's preface to the English edition

The process of learning a writing system has often been regarded as a simple matter of language instruction, providing the first steps into the schooling system, and, subsequently the State. But in my work, I explored it as a matter of linguistic ideology. When I started to write *A Voice for Maria Favela*, literacy education was not an exercise in learning and thinking, creating and living: instead, it was an empty exercise of repetition. Empty letters of empty words in empty structures – albeit with latent intent.

At that time, the first words encountered in the children's literacy primers were all in 'school-speak' ('the girl is pretty', 'the cow gives us milk', etc.), apparently harmless phrases that were already dividing the children's world into categories, rankings and dichotomies of utility, even before they were capable of understanding the message being conveyed.

By then, Paulo Freire had already published his *Pedagogy of the Oppressed* (1968); my own perception was that Freire's method was conceived primarily for the oppressed working class, a proletariat formed mainly of factory or farm workers, adults who were capable of organizing themselves in order to understand their condition and, in doing so, struggle against oppression. That reality was dramatically different from what I discovered in the Rocinha Favela: here, children were being labelled by the school apparatus as 'incapable of learning', and were bouncing between heavy domestic work and petty criminality. They were in poor health, had seen relatives killed by the police and lived with mothers who were either unemployed or working as maids for the Brazilian middle-class, in conditions amounting to slavery. Marxist theorists would refer to this class of people as the *lumpenproletariat*.

To those kids, this new 'school-speak' made little sense: what did it matter if the girl was pretty, when she was so hungry and unhappy? And there were no cows, let alone fresh milk.

My first objective with the kids was to disrupt the school's idea of repetition, by introducing theatrical and graphic games in the classroom. Then, we also disrupted the logocentric notion of alphabetization as a mere derivation of speech, as we experimented with music, painting, theatre and other media. And we recast the characters from the kids' primers, creating new ones that lived in the Favela – that understood what we were saying.

This new dynamic allowed for the kids to express themselves, their traumas and their excitement, and together we understood that writing was, among other things, a game – one that we could read as a song, as a drama, as drawing. One that we could reinvent from scratch to tell the story of *Maria Favela*.

While immersed in this creative experience, I had to fight the schooling system – from the manuals to directors and inspectors. I had to disobey. And by doing so, I also walked towards my own liberation as an educator. The idea of the school as a positivist temple of order and civic duty was very dear to the military dictatorship in Brazil (1964–1985), and dismantling this idea was a revolutionary need.

Today, the shadows of the military regime once again lie over Brazil and threaten the entire educational process. While the government names educators, artists and scientists as enemies of the state, of family and of morals, the Ministry of Education promotes the farce of a 'school without ideologies', imposing phonics as the standard method for alphabetization and handing the administration of public schools over to the military.

I cannot think of more timely circumstances for translating *Fala Maria Favela* into English, and for daring new practices of writing.

Antonio Leal

Translator's introduction

By Alexis Gibbs

On the fortieth anniversary of the events described in this book, its 'adventure' is reaching an English audience for the first time. The author's name will not be familiar to many readers outside of Brazil, nor does he have the stature of his peer and near-contemporary, Paulo Freire (1921– 1997). But this modest volume contains more by way of pedagogical stimulus than its discreet measure betrays. On one level, it is an account of the trials and tribulations facing one teacher charged with the enormous task of turning around the attainment levels for literacy amongst a group of overlooked students. On another level, it encompasses issues of literacy education, creativity, liberatory pedagogy, Special Educational Needs and language-learning that are rarely synthesized in such a unique fashion. The joy and promise of this book, to my mind, lies in witnessing these two levels nourish one another, in a self-reflexive exercise that brings about practical results and conceptual revaluations in equal measure. By way of an Introduction to the text, I will briefly touch on some of its key themes, as well as their translatability – both in terms of language and of culture.

The Author

Antonio Leal was born in Rio de Janeiro on 14 April 1944, to Portuguese immigrants. His parents, Alfredo and Albina, owned a small grocery store in a working-class neighbourhood, Madureira. Although his mother received little formal education, she encouraged Antonio, and his older brother Alfredo, to pursue university degrees. Alfredo became a lawyer and entered the diplomatic service, and Antonio obtained degrees in History, French and Law, with hopes of following his brother into diplomacy. However, with the military coup in 1964, these plans were abandoned, as his brother was serving in the Brazilian embassy in Moscow, making him an easy target for the regime. Instead, Antonio entered the guerrilla movement against the military government, as a member of the *Ação Libertadora Nacional* (National Liberation Movement).

The group was dissolved in 1974, and Leal became more involved in the cultural scene in Rio. He was already a member of the Teacher's Union, and in 1979 he participated in the organization of a major strike. The movement's leadership, including Leal, was arrested in August of that year, by the dictatorship's political police (DOPS). Leal even recalls a policeman threatening his life with the words: 'I will carry the wreath [at your funeral].'

Between 1979 and 1981, Leal won three national literary prizes in dramaturgy, having taken a position as a creative writing teacher at the Escolinha de Arte do Brasil. It was during this period that he documented the events of *Fala Maria Favela*, here translated in English as *A Voice for Maria Favela*. The first edition of the book was published by Leal and his wife, Graça, by their own press, Kizumba. Later, Attica – Brazil's largest educational publisher – acquired the rights and published many other editions. With *Fala Maria Favela*, Leal decided to pursue a career in higher education, and obtained a master's in pedagogy at the Fundação Getúlio Vargas. With the end of the military dictatorship, he and his family moved to a small village in the countryside, Tiradentes (Minas Gerais), then an effervescent cultural centre. There, they created an art and literacy cooperative school with other artists and educators.

Leal continued to produce and self-publish his work, and became a university professor: first at the Funrei university, and then at the Universidade Federal do Rio Grande do Norte, in Natal (Rio Grande do Norte), from which he retired in 2002.

The Favela

This brief biography provides important background to an understanding of a unique text, both in terms of its authorship and its translatability. When Antonio Leal ended up, in 1981, heading into the favela district of Rocinha, in Rio de Janeiro, to take on a class of 'unteachables' (a group of students who had failed to meet the required reading and writing standard three years running), his own extraordinary 'adventure' in literacy teaching began – and with it the task of the translator also.

The very first problem that a translator encounters when trying to do justice to the site and citizens that are the subjects of this book is the want of vocabulary in English without some form of value judgment attached. The *favela* of the book's title, for instance, is a reference to a place for which the English language has no adequate direct correlate: the options invariably involve words like 'shack', 'shanty', 'shanty town', 'slum', none of which share in the celebration of life that is to be found in the favelas, alongside its many hardships. The *favela* is not just a geographic, architectural or a socioeconomic descriptor; it is a place with its own vernacular, a culture within itself, a form of life. It exists both in the conscious and unconscious minds of its inhabitants.

By extension, the *favelado*, or citizen of the favela, also has a unique identity, one that can neither be defined by the politics of the time, nor in opposition to it. The word (for which Google Translate offers the more pejorative 'slum dweller') not only carries the objective meaning of someone *from* the favela, but also to some degree an adjectival sense of being 'favela-ed'. Which is to say that people from this background, as with any background, are immersed in it, and have its rules and codes of conduct inscribed into their being. It should not be assumed, therefore, that these are necessarily individuals who have a conscious desire to treat their *favelado* status as a political identity, one that can be marshalled to the educational cause of social awareness-raising. The *favelado/a* is as likely to be as fond of their home as they are to seek freedom from it. The *favela* is not something for the favelado/a to overcome, escape or transcend (though many may choose/want to do so); it is a fact of one's existence.

The upshot of the uniqueness and facticity of favela life means that its citizens don't just need *better* education: they demand a different kind of education, a different way of thinking about education. In Leal's words:

> The favela child is active, creative by nature, and lively. When confronted with an all-knowing educator, who belongs to a different social class and tries to mold the child according to the image of the more dominant class, the favela child becomes a mere passive observer and listener. When going to school, the favela child has to leave their world on the outside and adopt different manners and customs.

To submit to the school's demand for inauthenticity is deeply counterintuitive for the favela child. But this was the challenge that faced Antonio Leal when he arrived at the Escola Paula Brito, in that he felt a personal pedagogical responsibility to get these 'unteachable' children to the same basic level of literacy as their peers, whilst doing justice to the distinctiveness of his students and their background, and whilst also acknowledging his own outsider position in attempting to do so. Given the circumstances, many educators might have fallen back on the box of tools with which their training had provided them. But Leal embraces the 'nothing-to-lose' potential of the situation to take a closer look at what this particular group of students needs from him, instead of proceeding to try and fix them according to his own art or instrument.

One of his first tasks in this regard is to assess the immediate environment: not just the school, which has evidently taken on the microcosmic form of the broader military apparatus, but its backdrop of the Rocinha favela, which hums, thrives and survives in the near distance. Despite being labelled as having 'Special Educational Needs', Leal sees the students in his classroom not so much as deficient in their learning abilities, but as people who haven't mastered the inauthenticity of school-based learning, particularly when it assumes abstract shapes and forms whose value is only ever presented as self-evident. As a reaction against the abstract, monological character of the literacy curriculum and its associated methods, Leal immediately gets to work on engaging the aesthetics of the favela, the shapes and forms that emerge from its unique set of cultural attributes.

What becomes evident in this process is that Antonio Leal neither wants to Romanticize favela life, nor call for its dramatic overhaul. But he does insist on the value of its difference from other modes of city-dwelling, a difference that may well reside in the highly public character of its everyday life, as opposed to the increasingly private existences that metropolitans otherwise occupy. He discovers in this way of life an openness and integrity, even as he learns about the harsh and fractured lives of his individual students. At the same time, he doesn't play at being their protector, by trying to conceal or emolliate some of the harsher realities of the children's daily existence within their learning activities. The violence that is part of their everyday existence is part of their vocabulary also. In his words: 'It's important to talk about violence, in every classroom: representing and analyzing what is going on.' Representation affords recognition, and allows for the reality of young people's existence to filter into their learning, to help them come to terms with it and make sense of it in language. But this is why a standardized mode of written communication is also important, because otherwise people would only be able to make sense of their existence independently of others, rather than in relation to them. Here is where the process of *alfabetização* becomes significant.

Alfabetização

Another of the more important terms in this book also happens to be one of those instances in which we find that English doesn't have a very satisfactory direct translation of a word, despite it representing a key part of our educational vocabulary. We tend to take it for granted that literacy refers exclusively to the ability to read and write. But English doesn't have an equivalent word either for the Portuguese verb *alfabetizar* (to teach literacy to others), or the noun *alfabetização* (the process of becoming literate), whilst the adjective *alfabetizado* loses its past participle significance when translated simply as 'literate'. The active and passive positions inferred by these words do not obtain in their English counterparts in the same way: we would require something like the verb 'to literatize' to achieve the same effect.

At its more literal level, *alfabetização* most commonly refers strictly and specifically to the learning and mastery of the alphabet as a form of code, with little sense of semantics that some definitions of literacy might imply. The word is closer to Uta Frith's 'alphabetic' stage of reading acquisition: it has to do with memory and recognition, as opposed to interpretation and appreciation. Brazilian-Portuguese has another associated word for literacy which is 'letramento', a term which more fully encompasses the social dimensions of being able to read and write, including the application, understanding and use of words according to diverse situations. 'Letramento' – a relatively recent concept which began to take hold in Brazilian educational discourse around the time of Leal's classroom experiments – extends beyond the mere recognition of signs and symbols to an understanding and interpretation of them, and might therefore be considered a more sophisticated achievement of literacy.

Instead of departing from the dominant discourse, Antonio Leal chooses to operate within it, whilst challenging that dominance in an exploration of its plasticity. The use of the word 'alfabetização' becomes appropriated to his own design, and therefore makes matters more complex: he is at once describing the simple task of getting children to recognize individual letters as parts of a unitary system, whilst gradually formulating his own conception of teaching literacy as awarding meaning 'to each word through its individual expression and register, in significant ways'. Just as we speak of 'emotional literacy', 'visual literacy' and 'media literacy', so Leal draws attention to the different ways in which we might become 'alphabetized': through cinema, photography, literature. To extend the realm and range of this word, then, is not to reconceptualize it altogether. Consequently, *alfabetização* is also not to be understood, in Leal's text, as some kind of equivalent – or alternative – concept to Paul Freire's notion of *conscientização*. Indeed, *alfabetização* is the word used throughout Paulo Freire and Donaldo Macedo's *Alfabetização: Leitura do mundo, leitura da palavra* (*Literacy: Reading the Word and the World*, 1987), in which it comes to mean a relationship to reading and writing that explores and effects the subjective-objective critical awareness described earlier. Under this aegis, *alfabetização* moves dialectically from the assumption of a passive learner to the affirmation of an active one. For Leal, by contrast, *alfabetização* is both the simple fact of learning to read and write, *as well as* the capacity to imbue the world with meaningfulness through acts of reading and writing. His version acknowledges the logic of literacy, whilst infusing it with added layers of feeling, culture, imagination and voice. Again, this is not a way of politicizing the people of the favela, but a form of enabling people's agency within the realm of everyday life.

Alfabetização, then, is at once didactically banal and semantically complex. An effective translation therefore demands that this word come across at times as ordinary and familiar, and at other times as something almost strange. Leal achieves this double effect in his own text by constantly alluding to possibilities of meaning beyond the ordinary, but we have elected to use the words 'literate' and 'literacy' where a more procedural sense is implied, and the anglicized *alphabetize* and *alphabetized* where Leal's own inflection appears more appropriate. When it came to the subtitle of the book, for example, we opted for 'An Adventure in Creative Literacy' because the use of the word 'alphabetization' would have seemed too esoteric.

Creative Literacy

Leal's own development of a 'creative literacy' emerges initially out of reservations over whether the teaching of reading and writing need be either a didactic or a dialectical exercise. Leal recognizes from the outset that his pedagogical task is less to overthrow the system of codification altogether, and more to engage it from a different – and more meaningful – direction. This is the approach that Leal describes as 'creative', in that it is both playful and relational, drawing on different sources of inspiration to constantly rediscover the vitality of language. Elliot Eisner talks about literacy in a similar fashion:

> Language used in the service of the poetic is quite different than language used in the service of the literal. One can be literate in one form and illiterate in the other. What schools need to attend to are the cultivation of literacy in its many forms. Each form of literacy provides another way to be in the world, another way to form experience, another way to recover and express meaning.
>
> (Eisner, 2008: 27–8)

A creative approach to teaching literacy, or *alphabetizing*, can only succeed as a game that is both free and freeing, as enjoyment, as creativity, as meaningfulness and as fluidity.

To insist on *creative* literacy is to account for the liberatory force of becoming-literate, whilst remaining within its regulatory parameters. A creative pedagogy can only be liberatory if it presumes neither means nor ends, but instead works with the student to uncover both. The teacher must be 'willing to listen, as I was, and to really hear the students, to hear their music, their games, their stories – their culture, in fact – and goes further, freeing them, removing the censure placed on them such that their unconscious and their imagination is allowed free voice' (p.56).

The free voice (which we have awarded a place in the title of the book) is the goal of creative literacy, and it can be cultivated within the classroom, because even the most anarchic of conditions provides 'fertile ground for discovery and for creativity' (p.57). Here again the unconscious seems to play an important role, providing the disruptive energy that can become a source of discovery. This kind of force has significant political import: the events recounted in *A Voice for Maria Favela* took place in the final years of Brazil's military dictatorship, which came to an end in March 1985. By this time, the school system had been thoroughly infiltrated by what Leal calls the 'bureaucratic-civic-military apparatus', an entanglement of Kafka-esque protocols, operations and ideologies designed to reproduce the regime's values from the curriculum outwards. In essence, then, Leal's vision for literacy education under these conditions is one in which freedom through education is accomplished as a freedom against and from the bureaucratization and militarization of the school environment. These motions are what systematically exclude those members of society who can neither grasp nor master their self-evidence:

> here, to be illiterate, to lack means of expression – these are things that stand in the way of people's ability to communicate freely, because the system does not want them to, because the State does not want them to. Instead, violence distracts them, holds them back, prevents them from taking any kind of control over their lives.

Against this social repression, Leal advocates an approach that recognizes the emancipatory value of being able to read and write, whilst privileging the role of the artistic and the unconscious in achieving that emancipation.

Leal's interest in the conscious and unconscious processes that inform our meaningful and symbolic engagement with the world takes its cue from a wide variety of (often surprising) sources, almost all of which are linked by the association between art(istic practice) and expression. The Brazilian follower of Carl Jung, Nise de Silveira (1905–1999), for instance, was well known for favouring practices of getting patients to work with paint and sculpture over speech-based therapy, and her Museu de Imagens do Inconsciente (Museum of Images of the Unconscious) became a centre for research and subsequently exhibition that receives explicit mention as an influence on Leal's burgeoning work with children.

The development of an emphasis on the creative within the literacy process is at times reminiscent of those other educational thinkers who are concerned to reconcile the political with – and within – the aesthetic: Friedrich Schiller (1759–1805), John Dewey (1859–1952), Maxine Greene (1917–2014), Loris Malaguzzi (1920–1994) and Jacques Rancière (1940–). As a dramatist, Schiller's writings on aesthetic education provide important precedent here, not least because of their emphasis on harmonizing the competing forces of nature and reason, a dynamic that Schiller believed can only be achieved through play. These forces seem also to guide Leal's intuition around letters, that they must retain their social dynamism through individual expression. But another dramatist features even more prominently in Leal's frame of explicit reference: Augusto Boal, the Brazilian drama educator. Leal not only draws on Boal's ideas for some of his classroom activities, but is inspired to view the classroom as both the scene of politics and a stage. He employs techniques such as improvisation of scenes, and the rotation of roles within those scenes, to encourage a multi-perspectival and embodied understanding of language and its lived experience.

From the enactment and observation of the drama-based games, there emerges a revaluation of the role of play in learning to read and write. Play has been a common feature of literacy theory and practice since the nineteenth century, with Maria Montessori (1870–1952), Jean Piaget (1896–1980) and Lev Vygotsky (1896–1934) all affirming playful interactions with the world as beneficial in enhancing first-hand experience of letter and word usage. Leal's version of play pays special attention to the conditions and environment of the favela, not least the facts of its lack of privacy and therefore collectivity:

> Favela children in particular, can be seen to express all their wishes, their sexuality, their despair, matters of life and death, the entire *universe* in fact, through collective play.

The favela child comes into consciousness of a world that is largely unbounded, because everyone shares in one another's business and experience. But this does not mean a lack of individuation: each person has the potential to discover their identity within the collective, through self-exploration and creative re-imagining. Leal repeatedly returns to the notion that

> a mastery of one's own tongue is the route to personal strength and freedom; it is a journey that plunges us deep into the imagination, into the subconscious, into the cosmic, only to return us to the surface in a reconstruction of lines of thought and speech, a revaluation of the *favelas*, a confrontation with one's own image, and a creation of new alphabets in the process of learning to read and write!

Here is where Leal sounds most like another of his cited sources of influence, the artist Paul Klee (1879–1940), most notably in his emphasis on *line* in literacy (as opposed to letter), and on the act of creation (as opposed to instruction). Consider this passage from Klee's Notebooks on artistic practice:

> For the present then let us content ourselves with the most primitive of elements, the line. At the dawn of civilization, when writing and drawing were the same thing, it was the basic element. And as a rule our children begin with it; one day they discover the phenomenon of the mobile point, with what enthusiasm it is hard for us grown-ups to imagine. At first the pencil moves with extreme freedom, wherever it pleases.
>
> But once he begins to look at these first works, the child discovers that there are laws which govern his random efforts. Children who continue to take pleasure in the chaotic are, of course, no artists; other children will soon progress towards a certain order. Criticism sets in. The chaos of the first play-drawing gives way to the beginning of order. The free motion of the line is subordinated to anticipation of a final effect; cautiously the child begins to work with a very few lines. He is still primitive.
>
> (Klee, 1961: 103)

Leal shares with Klee a fascination with the primitive, and the idea that educators and artists need to keep reaching back towards a more primordial state to understand and appreciate the tools and instruments we take for granted today. They also have in common a belief in the necessity for giving order to an otherwise chaotic world through line and language. Leal says of Class 111 at one point that 'My task was to build order from chaos'. This is not just a requirement placed on the teacher, but it is a responsibility towards the student: to deprive them of the ability to make sense of the world through line and letter, is to deprive them of the ability to know and be known.

Mark-making, in particular, is returned to in Leal's process as the means by which humans can find order in the chaos of the world, with lines coming into being as both a form of communication and its trace. But rather than work with their contemporary, more complex forms, Leal chooses to return to more basic marks, such that the children in his class can build their understanding of the written word from more identifiable elements. It is here that Leal lights upon the ancient Chinese book of the I-Ching to provide him with the basic unit of literacy to attest to these dual components.

Leal's innovative use of the I Ching as a way to appeal to a basic understanding of building meaning through lines doesn't attempt to recreate anything of their significance within Chinese culture. Instead, the hexagrams are employed as a simple starting point:

> I could envision beginning with the hexagrams themselves, and then working with them as the building blocks for images, then symbols, and finally letters.

From here, the potential for weaving the *alphabetizing* process into a self-awareness process on the part of the students becomes more apparent:

> The path towards a new game of graphics lay open. What's more, I was beginning to get to know my students a little better by now, and I sensed a need to work both on their reclamation of identity as well as their group cohesion. We would have to entirely reconstruct the life-space in which they had been operating. This simple graphic game appeared to make that a possibility also.

The games that Leal devises for the children initially also often involve the use of lines. These lines are not just drawn, but form the basis for games, and are often seen to be an extension of the children's physical and active being; they are a mode of discovering agency.

Against Theory, against Method

Leal goes to great lengths to emphasize the fact that he is not writing a work of pedagogical theory. The story is written against the possibility of it becoming such a work, in that each new development gives cause for rethinking both the status quo of school-based learning and Special Education, as well as the author's own perceptions and preconceptions. It is open-ended, in style and in statement. Leal's own Introduction to the original text states that neither it, nor its ideas, are in a state of completion, but are 'a work in progress'. It would therefore be unwise to try and put a stamp on the precise nature and methodology of Leal's 'creative literacy'; it would be antithetical to the adventure his book describes. Indeed, if comparisons are to be made with Jacques Rancière's *Ignorant Schoolmaster* (1991), they are perhaps better drawn with the figure of Joseph Jacotot (1770–1840) in that book than with Rancière himself. After all, Leal is to be judged more on the example that he sets, than on the theoretical position he expounds.

To take such a strong stance against both theory and method clearly has one main objective: to do justice to the child. If children are themselves works in progress, and their unconscious minds are precisely what prevents against our having access to their specific (political) requirements, then no amount of theorising as to their true nature, their developmental abilities, the aims of their education, can adequately account for the vast range of needs and differences with which they (individually) present. What's more, the narrative in *A Voice for Maria Favela* does not arrive at any point of prescription: it cannot do more than describe the steps taken, and the outcomes achieved as a result. In this, it is closer to an experiment in good intentions, than it is to a work of theory. For some of the students, the experiment becomes a story of success; for others, however, life gets the better of them.

Whilst Leal doesn't provide the reader with a manual for a creative literacy, his contribution to educational thought comes to us more by way of a personal lexicon, or a revisiting of language in the light of present concerns, as opposed to universal ideas: literacy, experience, games, play, method, student, community, etc. In his words:

> The terms I am using here are by no means either critically, or conceptually, definitive. On the contrary, I have given them my own meanings, but each reader should also be in search of his or her own alphabet, and should give his or her own meaning to each of these terms.

The use of ordinary terms, accompanied by his own deliberate inflections, is consistent with the creative approach he is assuming and exploring throughout, hence the description of them as his own personal 'alphabet'. All these words are re-visited for the influence (if not a kind of captivity) that their standard usage holds over us, and how we, as educators and educationalists, might be empowered to see our conceptual language as something to which we ascribe meaning, as well as having it handed to us.

When turning to children as the subjects of education, it is not simply a matter of making the world meaningful on the educator's terms, but encouraging children to see themselves as part of a world that is already replete with language as representation:

> Each person must be understood as a whole. We have to look closely at each person's modes of representation and self-representation, which are sought deep within their being. We need to look closely at their many languages.

The 'many-languagedness' of our individual being referred to here is redolent of both Loris Malaguzzi's later work, *The 100 Languages of Children* (published in 1993), and Russian literary theorist Mikhail Bakhtin's (1895-1975) concept of dialogism, the celebration of the fact that any one person is both born into and capable of assuming a plurality of discourses, whilst still achieving a wholeness of being via their exploration and expression. Bakhtinian dialogue is perhaps best understood in terms of what it is not, that is its antithesis, dialectics:

> Take dialogue and remove the voices (the partitioning of voices), remove the intonations (emotional and individualizing ones), carve out abstract concepts and judgments from living words and responses, cram everything into one abstract consciousness – and that's how you get dialectics.
>
> (Bakhtin, 1986: 147)

Dialectical approaches to thinking about language risk taking the life from it. Bakhtin, like Leal, sensed that no problem was ever as simple as setting one side up against another, because even within the individual there are too many 'voices' and 'intonations' and 'judgments' all jostling for their utterance – let alone within groups of people (such as the favelados). Against the universalization and abstraction of dialectics, both Bakhtin and Leal celebrate multiplicity, ephemerality and the carnivalesque. But whilst the carnival in Bakhtin remains a heavily theorized term, for Leal it is part of the lived experience of his students, and key to understanding their way of life.

Method, then, is only useful in its humility: 'The important thing is to create a method for every experience,' Leal writes, and they should be seen as 'disposable objects that you use once and then throw away'. What is so distinctive about *A Voice for Maria Favela* is its refusal to present itself as method; instead, the text enacts the author's attitude *toward* method, which is to say that it can only be situational, provisional, relational and dialogical. To appreciate the ways in which this approach might translate into other circumstances, requires the kind of sensibility and – to use Elliot Eisner's expression – 'educational connoisseurship' that allow us to adapt games, play, skills and techniques to the time and place of learning.

In short, Leal provides his reader not with instruction but with example. Stories such as this one need to be told, because they provide us with possibilities and alternatives for creative approaches to pedagogy. They also remind us of the limitations of what can be achieved in practice. The world of theory is one in which things will always work, as long as they are carried out exactly according to theoretical dictate. The world of practice is one in which things don't always work, errors abound, and an ever-attentive sensibility for how things might be done differently is required, particularly when our theoretical expectations fall short. Leal's adventure affords primacy to this sensibility so that we don't become de-sensitized to the needs of the people we teach, adopting 'modes of literacy that are by turns mechanical, repetitive, alienating, stereotyping, and so on'.

Leal and Freire

Leal's book was written very much in the wake and awareness of Paulo Freire's (1921–1997) achievements in the fields of critical and emancipatory pedagogy,[1] but *A Voice for Maria Favela* was not written either in response or in opposition to Freire's critical pedagogy. Leal pays tribute to the influence of Freire through an evident appreciation of his work throughout, rather than through a direct application of it. Whilst he views the latter as being fatal to doing justice to the particularities of his own pedagogical situation, the former enriches both his understanding and vocabulary in relation to that situation.

Freire's greatest achievement was to draw attention to the ways in which educational processes reproduced social, political and epistemological injustices via the oppressive and prescriptive architecture of the curriculum. What Leal and Freire share most in common, then, is the orientation of pedagogy towards freedom. In Freire, this takes the form of a literacy that must account both for the individual learner's history, experience, economic status and cultural background, and for the dominant culture's codification of learning, such that the former can transcend the latter. The consciousness-raising efforts entailed in this mode of literacy are necessarily premised not only upon fundamental tensions between the subject and the objectivity of the social sphere, but also upon a false consciousness on the part of the learner: social awareness cannot be achieved until we are aware of the illusoriness of our given reality. To effect this change, literacy must also be a conceptually blunt instrument: reading and writing are part of the social practices of reality, and therefore subjective experiences of culture must be called upon to place them into context. On this view, reading the word enables a reading of the world. Freire does not really explore the possibilities of creative transformation from *within* the alphabet, seeing literacy skills more as means to the end of world engagement and social change. By contrast, the horizon of Leal's literacy-learning is not the 'world'

---

[1] Freire's *Pedagogy of the Oppressed* was published some thirteen years previously, and Leal and Freire were personally acquainted with one another.

of global citizenship, but the world of a person's immediate environment: the freedom he seeks to cultivate is an agency within one's own surrounds.

Some might argue that this vision lacks ambition, particularly when learners remain structurally disenfranchised because of their cultural background. Emancipation, on this view, must mean freedom from oppression. But Leal is reluctant to assume oppressed status on the part of his pupils; the people he sees before him in the classroom are individuals with a right to self-control in their existence, but should not be thought of as oppressed according to a rule – not least because the mind of the child, in its conscious and unconscious operations, cannot be contained by the adult's understanding of it. The key to freedom doesn't lie with the educator, therefore: only through play can the child reveal and discover their potential. Leal's concern, then, as we have seen, is less with materiality and more with creativity.

This is not to deny the aesthetic dimensions to Freirean pedagogy. Tyson Lewis (2012) has written of Freire's attentiveness to audio-visual dimensions to the classroom experience, and the structures and hierarchies of inclusion and exclusion that a multi-sensory approach to teaching exposes. But Leal's account achieves something different, an aesthetics of practice in which an attentiveness to the task and individuals in hand showed that the classroom always holds surprises and unanticipated circumstances, and that the teacher's job is to identify and adapt. Once again, there is an echo of Eisner here, for whom educational connoisseurship means 'refining the levels of apprehension of the qualities that pervade classrooms' (Eisner, 2005: 40).

A Voice for Maria Favela Today

But can connoisseurship provide a sufficient rationale for bringing an otherwise obscure text to the awareness of a wider audience today? Why resurrect a Brazilian text from the 1980s now, when the educational times, contexts, language and concepts will all have moved on significantly, both in Brazil itself and globally? To see how this work might translate into other contexts requires some imagination, not only to think about creative literacies according to Leal's approach, but also to adapt them to our own purposes and design. There are a number of ways in which creative literacy might be understood as being of enduring relevance for educationalist and educator alike today.

Firstly, the symbiosis of the aesthetic and the political, the potential for creativity and art to engage young people with their world in new and exciting ways, has not gone away. The internet age has introduced both challenges and obstacles to young people's alphabetization: they are exposed to images, media and code in ways that this book could not have foreseen, and many find themselves more fluent in these languages than older generations. But there is increasing evidence that the emotional literacy required to navigate these new languages is not integrated into formal education; at the same time, the localized idioms that provide children with a sense of groundedness in their own culture are in many parts of the world at risk of being washed away by the tides of a universal digital language. The affirmation of emotional engagement as well as cultural heritage can inform the process of creative literacy as much as social struggle and individual agency.

Secondly, exemplarity. As has already been suggested, good theorizing exists in abundance in educational research, but good examples less so. And even if many teachers will struggle to see in *A Voice for Maria Favela* the potential for their own practice to take the same kind of risks, because of structural and bureaucratic constraints, they might still be persuaded to find in this narrative the encouragement to think differently about the foundations of those constraints, and how they might be challenged.

Finally, commonality. One of the difficulties faced by educators in multicultural classrooms today is that there can be little guarantee of a shared minimum culture between and across students, hence why much of the theorizing of the past twenty years has tended to think more in terms of difference than sameness. Leal's book may seem a little retrograde in this regard, given its tendency to think in terms of a community, and to assume that everyone within that community has something in common. But *A Voice for Maria Favela* shows that commonality need not rest entirely with matters of identity (though these will play a significant role): music, theatre, imagination, play, games, song, struggle, violence, fear – these are all things that learners can have in common also. To begin to find a voice for learners left on the margins of language, is to allow them to reveal those aspects of their existence which they share and are shareable amongst others.

The Translation

In their translators' Introduction to Célestin Freinet's *Cooperative Learning and Social Change*, David Clanfield and John Sivell note that 'Freinet was not an academic and so his writing is mercifully free of Eduspeak and other forms of professional jargon' (1990: ix). Antonio Leal, despite working at times in universities, was also not a career academic, and *A Voice for Maria Favela* was written before he completed his master's thesis. Its readers will therefore find themselves equally relieved, in this book, of that brand of 'Eduspeak' that might detract from the immanence of the prose and the experiences it describes.

But that is not to say that translating a book like this is without its challenges, and certainly the exercise brings home what very different languages Brazilian-Portuguese and English are. In particular, the musicality of the original is difficult to convey. Leal deliberately tries to infuse his classroom with the rhythms of the favela, to provide the children with continuity of place and space. As a result, his writing is similarly rhythmic, capturing both the sounds he hoped to recreate, and the responses he received. Spoken English is not as musical a language as Brazilian-Portuguese anyway, but it is even harder to reproduce the beats and syncopations of this work authentically, without it sounding affected. Instead, we have held to the book's simplicity and clear affinity for the child's point of view, when trying to communicate its sense of discovery, of curiosity, and of adventure. All of this means that the literacy process described is one in which every letter and word is carefully chosen for its familiarity, its sonority and its social resonance. Take, for instance, the title of the book in Brazilian-Portuguese: *Fala Maria Favela*. The title refers to one of the first complete phrases that the children put together, having started to identify sounds with lines as (capitalized) letters. But the phrase is not simply a matter of convenience: not only does each component hold political significance (whereby a recognizable individual, 'Maria', is metonymic for the children's own mothers and their struggles), but is comprised of a particular rhythm: FA-LA MA-Ri-A FA-Ve-LA. The phrase is easily sung and clapped, but not so easily translated. We have opted more for the political resonance simply to give it its political significance, highlighting the fact that the process the children go through is one of giving voice to the people of their own upbringing and background.

In those sections of the text which list the words given to the children as part of their evolving vocabulary, we have provided readers with both the original words, and their literal translations into English. This is in part to show how words were selected for their particular vowels and consonants, but also to afford the reader some impression of how that selection was intended to fuse sound with place, in words that were familiar and colloquial.

Aspects of prose style have also been adapted for this translation. This is not just to do with Brazilian-Portuguese having a different syntactical and grammatical coherence to English – Leal's own style and narrative in the original are also anything but linear: the storytelling is often desultory, and contains digressions, ellipses, non sequiturs, and observations that end inconclusively. The reader is warned early on that 'the tone of the book is without a sense of finality, or definitiveness'. Leal writes as if he were thinking in real time, thoughts still in formulation. Further, both tone and style are intended to be (unacademically) dialogical: at times Leal is in conversation with himself, at others he addresses his readers directly. Often, as with the hexagrams from which his adventure departs, he seems almost to interrupt one line of thought with another, less as a display of distractedness and more as an exercise in authenticity. Our lives, like our thoughts and our script, are not composed in one consecutive line: they pause, draw breath, dwell and deliberate. They are bisected by events, and intersected by other lives. Whilst we have tidied up some of the more raw edges to the original text, we have elected to preserve as much of the stylistic approach as possible. This may frustrate some readers, but it is again a necessary reflection both of the loose ends that teaching entails, and of a mode of inquiry that refuses to tie up those loose ends to provide easy solutions to complex contexts.

As a result, it is important to affirm once more that there has been no intention to present this work as one with any kind of universal application. Its contextual specificity resists that possibility at every turn. Rather, what the book invites is a call to attentiveness in the teaching situation, the development of a peculiar sensibility for responding pedagogically to contextual and contingent circumstance. It seems as essential to Leal's work, as it was for Klee, that 'The power of creativity cannot be named' – after all, the word creativity is noteably absent from Leal's 'alphabet'. But even if that power remains without a name, it may still be possible, as Maria Favela demonstrates, for it to find a voice.

References

Bakhtin, M. M. (1986). *Speech Genres and Other Late Essays.* Austin, TX: University of Texas Press.
Eisner, E. (2005). *Reimagining Schools: Selected Works of Elliot W. Eisner*. Abingdon: Routledge.
Eisner, E. (2008). 'What Education Can Learn from the Arts'. *LEARNing Landscapes* | Volume 2, Number 1, Autumn 2008. pp. 23–30.
Frith, U. (1985). 'Beneath the Surface of Developmental Dyslexia'. In K. E. Patterson, J. C. Marshall & M. Coltheart (Eds.) (pp. 301–30). London: Lawrence Erlbaum.

Klee, P. (1961). *Paul Klee Notebooks. Volume 1. The Thinking Eye*. London: Lund Humphries.

Lewis, T. (2012). *The Aesthetics of Education: Theatre, Curiosity and Politics in the Work of Jacques Rancière and Paulo Freire*. London: Continuum.

Rancière, J. (1991). *The Ignorant Schoolmaster: Five Lessons in Intellectual Emancipation*. Stanford, CA: Stanford University Press.

Introduction

The story behind this book has its origins in some work that I began in 1981, with a group of students classed as requiring 'Special Education' – that is to say, students who had spent more than three years in school, but had still not learned to read or write. The events took place at a public school, the Escola Paula Brito, in the Rocinha favela of Rio de Janeiro.

I had already been teaching in Rocinha since 1977, doing drama with young people. This work had resulted in a play called 'Where is Beto?', with words and music created by the students themselves. Throughout 1978 and 1979, I busied myself locally with other similar cultural projects, and it wasn't until 1980 that I fully committed to teaching at Paula Brito. Between June and December of that year, I attempted to get an initial impression of the school by trying out a number of different activities there: following the progress of a Special Education class, creating a small theatre group, researching the music of the favelas, and observing the well-known games and kinds of play among the children.

It was only once I had digested all these different aspects to the school environment and the lives of its students, that in 1981 I felt the need to steer my work onto a more definite path, one with fewer diversions and distractions. I decided to focus on basic literacy. At that time, I was already pretty clear in my own mind about what it meant to 'become literate'. I felt that I had already achieved a new kind of literacy myself over the course of many years as a novice writer, through the language of the theatre, of the cinema and also of literature. So the great adventure of reading and writing, of helping others to become literate – to be discoverers of the written word, artisans of language – was extremely exciting. It was in this spirit of discovery that I suggested to the Head of the school that I take responsibility for a literacy class. Ideally, I was looking to put together a special class of former students from my recent years on work placement, students said to be incapable of learning, and had therefore been sidelined within their own school.

The school at that time badly needed concrete evidence of change. Everyone was so tired of reforms and superstructural developments that the governors of the school district, and of the school itself, accepted my offer and in the process removed a number of the bureaucratic obstacles that might well have got in the way.

So much for context – let me say something about the structure of this story. Although the book is intended to be a patchwork of experiences, discoveries and opinions, peppered with incident and personal insight, it does also have an underlying logic: from within it emerges the design that underpinned the content of the classes themselves. It is at once its own primer, with numbered pages like any other, as well as a commentary on the processes I went through, which is at times a true-to-life diary of the class, and at others an account of the entire school, its scope widening with every new development. Finally, this book is also a glossary – or personal 'alphabet' – of words put together by the author, words which he has given particular meanings, and which guide his ideas. They are words which reveal how the author himself is still in the process of becoming literate; they are *literatizing* words.

The first of these words that I want to introduce here is the very first word that I, in documenting these events, sought to find a meaning for:

'Alfabetizar' (Teaching Literacy)

To teach someone to read and write is in a sense 'to alphabetize', to enable them to award meaning to each word through its individual expression and register, in significant ways. Both writing and drawing are primordial and ancient forms of representation which exist such that people might reproduce them – not as some form of lifeless code, complete and pre-packaged, but as breath, as spoken word, as creation and as handicraft.

Any word is but a footprint, a trace, a mark that man has elevated to something quintessential. The Latin alphabet, unlike the ideogram, does not directly connect the word to the thing; it is abstract. The thing emerges from a combination of script and sound, not as a reflection of an image.

Meanings are created from a thousand and one associations. For a child just leaving nursery school, the forceful yoking of written words to 'real' things is something they consciously reject. Children want games. A creative approach to teaching literacy, or *alphabetizing*, can only succeed as a game that is both free and freeing, as enjoyment, as creativity, as meaningfulness and as fluidity.

Words must be at times thrown in the air, and at others wrapped around us tight as a cloak. But there are so many obstacles to achieving this free play of spontaneity and control: consciousness, the human capacity for abstraction, the school, *the system*. The truth is that the system is afraid of a person's creative potential, their power to create language. This is even more of an issue for those that come from the favelas: here, to be illiterate, to lack means of expression – these are things that stand in the way of people's ability to communicate freely, because the system does not want them to, because the State does not want them to. Instead, violence distracts them, holds them back, prevents them from taking any kind of control over their lives.

Language is the key to this control: a mastery of one's own tongue is the route to personal strength and freedom; it is a journey that plunges us deep into the imagination, into the subconscious, into the cosmic, only to return us to the surface in a reconstruction of lines of thought and speech, a revaluation of the *favelas*, a confrontation with one's own image, and a creation of new alphabets in the process of learning to read and write!

> Q: But does teaching literacy not just amount to an indoctrination in the art of language manipulation?
> A: We can teach a literacy of the spoken word, through the creation of new written words.

And there are other literacies besides:

> There is *cinema literacy*, reading 24 frames per second.
> There is *photographic literacy*.
> There is *theatre literacy*.

Another word I believe to be important in my own 'alphabet' is:

Experience

Concrete experience is not something that has a start and end point, as is often thought. It is never fully 'done and dusted', 'tried and tested', 'over and done with'. The way I understand it, experience is something that is both lived and a way of living; it is a political practice.

It is a way of living because at no point can it be separated from any other part of one's life, it cannot be compartmentalized. Any one experience is part of all the others, forming an organic whole of lived behaviour.

Experience cannot be reduced to professional existence. It is life itself: alive, lived, vivid. Experience is always at the same time transformation.

Experience is politics in practice: it is the discovery of the new, brought into harmony with action. It is not the practice of a partisan politics, which always carries its own primers and catechisms. It is the enduring practice of self-liberation.

Experience shouldn't be thought of as an incident in isolation: we should always be looking for ways to reflect, to exchange and to critique, all as part of the same process. And we should be looking to make new connections, and discovering new spaces in which to make them – to advance knowledge from experience!

The terms I am using here are by no means either critically, or conceptually, definitive. On the contrary. I have given them my own meanings, but each reader should also be in search of his or her own alphabet, and should give his or her own meaning to each of these terms. To this end, the tone of the book is without a sense of finality, or definitiveness. I would even go so far as to say that this text reflects the very pleasure I take in writing: at times, its tone is almost literary.

As I have said, this book and the ideas it contains are by no means in a state of completion. Perhaps they will be one day? For the time being, this is a work in progress.

March of '81

I have the list of students in my hand: class 111. They are a group of twenty-six kids, aged from nine to eleven.

'Mr Leal, we have put in your class the school's two biggest troublemakers: José Carlos and Alexandre Alves'.

I'm not familiar with even one specific technique for teaching literacy. Not one. How am I going to do this? I'd read what I could of Paulo Freire, *The Pedagogy of the Oppressed* and *Education as the Practice of Freedom*, books that I had at home. And I'd read a book by Freinet on public education. But I still felt none the wiser, only assured of what I already knew to be the case, which was that there is simply no fool-proof formula for those that want to do something entirely different. Paulo Freire and Freinet just weren't coming up with the answers I needed.

Class was beginning. My students awaited me, lined up in the courtyard.

'Hey, check it out, the teacher is a *man*!'
'*Tio, tio* ... are you going to be our teacher?'[1]
'I am, yes. Let's go.'

It was the last classroom on the top floor.

From the Venetian windows, filled with broken glass, you could look into the houses climbing the hillside: television sets, imitation leather sofas, pictures of Saint George and Saint Sebastian, etc. Always a lot of children playing, flying kites, fights and chatter between husband and wife, men building new shacks... In short, the life of the favela drifted in through the classroom window. It permeated the life of the school, just as it should.

The classroom itself was always the same: individual desks, the teacher's table at the front, and the blackboard behind that.

The kids were all sat there, staring at me. They wanted to learn, were anxious to begin, eyes full of a trusting wonderment. I would need to unharden my heart if I was going to learn from them.

'My name is Leal, Mr Leal.'

I wanted to get to know them. I called them by name, but they never stopped calling me Sir, or Mr Leal, or *Tio*, even though I always wanted them just to call me Leal.

One of the first things I learned about these kids was that, despite having been in the same class for a number of years now, they still didn't know each other's names. This was bad. My first day, as I recall it, was therefore spent playing around with the sounds of people's names:

'I want you to close your eyes, and one by one say your name, first softly, and then louder, and louder, and louder ...'

Some shouted out their names, others whispered, others clammed up altogether, and some didn't even bother to shut their eyes.

'OK. Now, I want you to say the first sound of your name ...'

Once again, some of the kids remained silent (Alexandra, Adriana, Sônia, Ronaldo, José Edmílson). Others continued to shout out sounds excitedly: (Alexandre Alves, José Carlos, Clodoaldo).

We then chatted a bit about families: father, mother, how many siblings, what Dad does for a living, what Mum does for a living, who takes care of the house, how many of the kids are working, etc. They in turn were curious to know if I was married, if I had children.

---

[1] *Tio* is an informal mode of address for an older man, literally meaning 'Uncle'.

I also remember that in that class I decided to do a drawing task with them. I drew a series of lines on the board, writing at one end of each line the name of a student, and at the other end their initials.

A lot of the children were able to identify their own name, despite not knowing how to write it. At any rate, all of the names were identified. I asked them to pay special attention to their names; then I wiped all the letters from the board, leaving only the lines.

'Whose is this line?'
'Alexandre'
'And this one?'
'Rivelino'

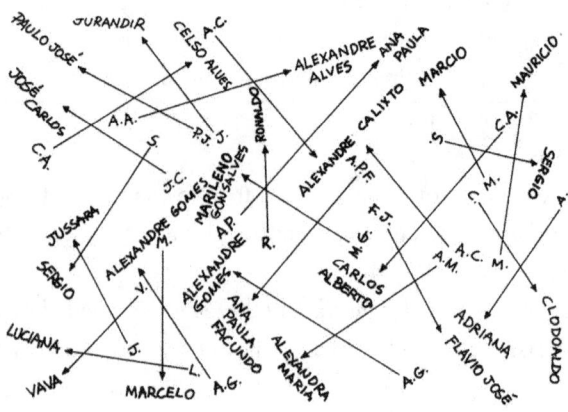

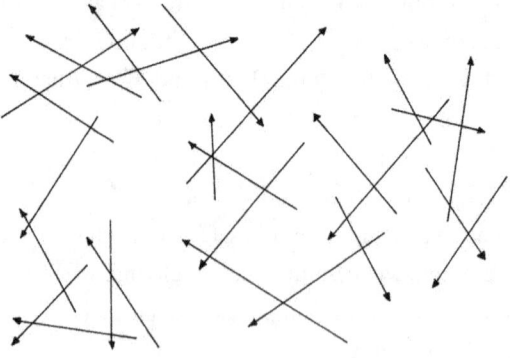

And so on and so forth. Every member of Class 111 was there, in amongst those criss-crossing lines. And they all got it.

I am not about to relate here every last detail of what went on in those classes, nor expound a lengthy lecture on teaching literacy, documenting all the exercises I used. This story will be limited to those significant findings in the gradual structuring of the experience, backed up by my own thoughts and opinions, which developed over the course of my time with the students. In this respect, it could be noted that the observation on 'becoming literate' which opens this book came to me almost as soon as the school year had begun, at the moment I first came into contact with the spelling primers and other material used by those teaching reading and writing at the school. They spurred me into thinking about what have come to be some of the basic conclusions of this book:

1. That our alphabet is abstract, and has nothing figurative about it. The word 'table' bears no resemblance to a table; nor the word 'school', to a school.
2. We shouldn't link a word to a drawing of that thing. This just confuses the matter.
3. The alphabet is not purely formal and entirely separate from its creator. It is a profound manifestation of one's own being, and should be constantly performed as such.

Soon into my first class I realized something: the handwritten cursive script is difficult to write and to decipher. I believe that any code we all have in common should be legible.

These were all issues that became the subject of long conversations I had with my wife,[2] and with the artist Fernando Barata,[3] and with other friends. In his work, Fernando used lines that sought out an expression of the primitive through drawing, developing a 'true alphabet'. I started to think that it might be important to get the children to draw. I began reading a book on Chinese ideograms put together by Humberto de Campos.[4] I then went in search of a few

---

[2] Graça Leal (1949–), Art Educator.
[3] Fernando Barata (1961–), Brazilian painter and designer.
[4] Humberto de Campos Veras (1886–1934): Brazilian journalist, politician and writer. The book referred to here is Humberto de Campos (ed.), *Ideograma: Lógica, Poesia, Linguagem*, Cultrix, 1977.

articles about graphology in the *Humboldt* magazine.⁵ I read, with great interest, a collection of texts on constructivism, which was accompanied by abundant examples from poetry, sculpture, Bauhaus architecture and conceptual art. Another book that I looked at out of curiosity was the psychiatrist Nise da Silveira's book, *The Museum of the Unconscious.*⁶

But let's get back to Class 111 …

After more than three years of trying to read and not succeeding, the kids were arriving in class tired of carrying around their bags full of books, notebooks, scissors, rulers and primers. I understood the uselessness of all this stuff.

I took them to play out on the patio of the fourth floor.

'Play however you please', I told them.

The space was fairly big and was also being used as a dumping ground for unwanted chairs, tables and cupboards. But the proposal that they should play as they please had caught the kids off guard; school was not somewhere for them to play freely, or even a place to play at all. They had plenty of ideas for games, but immediately disagreed over them, unable to choose any one game that they all wanted to play. They then separated into smaller groups: some broke into fights, others just started running about the place, others remained in the corners, and others beat the cupboards with pieces of wood. Alexandra didn't want to play at all. In short, I was witnessing boys and girls who were normally quite accustomed to organizing their own games in the favela, unable to do so at school.

With some effort, I managed to get them back together in the middle of the terrace and suggested that we have a sing-along in a circle. The song went like this:

O Circo pegou fogo	*The circus caught on fire*
São Francisco deu o sinal	*And St Francis gave the sign*
Acuda, acuda, acuda	*Rescue, rescue, rescue*
A Bandeira Nacional	*The flag of the nation:*
Brasil!!!	*Brazil!!!*

When they said 'Brazil!' they would have to stop and remain completely still.

The kids already knew this game. From their frozen positions, they were then allowed to relax.

---

⁵ Physical Geography and Environmental Magazine, official journal of the Department of Physical Geography and Post-Graduate Programmes of the Institute of Geography at the Universidade de Estado do Rio do Janeiro (UERJ).

⁶ Nise da Silveira (1905–1999) was a Brazilian psychiatrist and a student of Carl Jung.

It's important in situations like this to begin with games that the children already know, and then from there to devise the games that they want, with objectives that they themselves have created. But first I needed to calm them down, and this game provided the perfect opportunity for relaxation.

We continued to play in a circle, with the last exercise being the following: everyone linked hands as a group, and one boy stepped outside of the circle in order to try and re-enter, but the others would have to prevent him at all costs. But with the very first attempt to penetrate the circle, the children disbanded – and from there it was impossible to get them back together.

Back in the classroom, I dispensed with their usual class materials, and gave each child just a pencil and a piece of white paper. I told them to draw their signature – not in the form of a sequence of letters, but just as a visual representation of their name.

Next, I split them into about six groups of four students, giving each group a sheet of white card. I told them that they should all draw a single line, using the full extent of the piece of card, a line that had to mix with the lines of their fellow students, such that they crossed but did not break up in the process.

At the end of the lesson, we sat once again in a circle and took stock of what we'd done that day and the day before. I felt this to be important, making sure that every one of the class's events remained alive in their memories.

From then on, we would always set aside time in our lessons for play, time for some form of drawing game, time to eat and time to talk about what had happened that day.

Games and play must always constitute the point of departure...

Play

Playing is the first real sign of childhood, and should be taken into account not only when it comes to literacy classes, but in all the early stages. Favela children in particular can be seen to express all their wishes, their sexuality, their despair, matters of life and death – the entire universe, in fact – through collective play.

The lack of space in any favela dwelling, a rigid if not authoritarian family structure, and the frequent absence of either mother or father can make it almost impossible for a child to explore more individualized forms of playful expression. These require a level of concentration and attention on the part of child, adult and entire household. As a result, most games are played outside, and are developed in collective spaces. Any game that I can recall from my childhood that I have seen replayed in the favelas will have a vast number of variations on the original, and with many more meanings to it also. I have witnessed almost twenty ways to Leapfrog, and innumerable versions of Hide-and-Seek, of Tag, of Cops and Robbers, of 'Vivo-Morto'.[7] And I noticed that, if left to their own devices, these young people were perfectly capable of getting themselves organized and following common rules. At school, meanwhile, they became completely paralysed, the instinct for gameplaying taken from them; beneath the censure or watchful gaze of a teacher, they lost all spontaneity.

Games

A *game*, as I understand it, is something different to *play*: a game must have a stated aim, a course of action, and an underlying rationalization of what might otherwise be too nebulous, or remain too fluid. It also seemed to me that, if our goal were to come up with a series of games, then it would be particularly important to ensure that the links and connections between them be clear and reinforced, and that we could retrace the history of their development. A dramatic work functions in the same way – in fact, a dramatic work is much like a primordial game. All literacy teachers should really take a course in theatre so as to have experienced these games: there lies in them the necessary skill for opening up of the space, the loosening of one's limbs, of one's voice, sound itself.

Every teacher ought to have as a point of reference the 200 drama games of Augusto Boal.[8]

The game is what launches every individual onto the path of self-discovery as a complete being: head, torso and limbs, the conscious and unconscious mind, animal and spirit, the imaginary, the mystery... Life can only be built from the knowledge of these as a totality.

---

[7] Literally translating as 'Alive-Dead, Dead-Alive', a children's game that is similar to musical statues: someone shouts the command of either 'Dead!' or 'Alive!' and the children have to either stand up (Alive) or crouch down (Dead) according to the command. If they move incorrectly according to the command, they are eliminated.

[8] Augusto Boal (1931–2009) Brazilian theatre practitioner, drama theorist and political activist, whose ideas were profoundly influenced by Paulo Freire. The games referred to here are found in Augusto Boal, *200 Exercícios e Jogos para o Ator e o Não Ator com Vontade de Dizer Algo Através do Teatro*, Rio de Janeiro: Civilização Brasileira, 1977.

Of course, we can't work with games in the same way that we do with primers. A teacher who doesn't have their head screwed on can't work with games. Those who are unsure fear any kind of changeability, and to work with games (the 'ludic') means to work with the changeable.

Spontaneous gameplaying, a theatrical game, a game-within-the-game – all these involve unforeseen paths that can only be explored by the creative teacher.

I got back to organizing the pupils into groups of four. I gave each group a differently coloured piece of paper. I asked each member of the group to draw a line in pencil, crossing over the lines of the others until they reached the far side of the paper. At the edge of the piece of paper, we stapled a large piece of string to the end point of each of the lines drawn. The idea was as follows: each child would have their own piece of string, and they would have to wrap the string around themselves and the others in their group without getting tied up. The ends of all the pieces of string from all the groups would then be tied to the same point on the ball of string. One of the students, Alexandre Gomes, would then be tasked with binding all the groups by one single thread. With the operation over, they would then have to release themselves from the string and return to their tables where their original piece of paper lay.

Need I say what really happened? Feeling themselves trapped by the threads, which were getting wrapped around their legs, hands, necks, torsos, the kids soon gave up and started to tug on their own bit of thread, and squeezing their partners in the process. There were moments of panic. Some of them got hurt, others cut themselves loose in frustration. The pieces of paper all got torn up. No one managed to return to their own group.

I repeated a lot of these exercises, whether it was getting the kids to be bound together, or build favelas out of string and plastic and waste paper. They began to get the idea: if you aren't careful, you risk hurting others. And frequently I was the one left feeling hurt...

A lot of the kids still preferred not to take part in these games and remained aloof: Jussara, Sônia, Alexandra and José Edmílson. Always the same kids.

At the end of one class in March, Adriana said to me, 'Mr Leal, tomorrow is Jussara's birthday'.

'Is that true, Jussara? Why doesn't someone bring along a cake?'

And so it was decided: Clodoaldo, Alexandre Alves, Ana Paula and Celso would all bring the drinks, and the birthday girl would bring the cake.

Jussara's was the first birthday to be celebrated in that classroom.

And I, meanwhile, thought more and more about writing, what it means to write...

Before arriving at the alphabet itself, a person should have mastered many semiotic systems, many primitive scripts, many rituals, many handwritten codes – signs before sentences. This idea had me thinking.

Another thing I dwelt on a lot was the idea that writing ought to be an act of pleasure. Writing is drawing. But writing comes *before* literacy. A child of three or four years of age begins to write without knowing a single letter.

Where should I begin, then, in giving shape to the lines that the children had already begun drawing? What road should I be taking? One week of classes had gone by and I still knew nothing. Or I knew just one thing: I didn't want to apply the conventional methods, that would simply ask the students to copy, like a mode of housetraining. Please no, anything but that.

Methods

What sort of method should a literacy teacher follow? A word-based literacy – 'wordification' – begins by looking at the basic component parts of words, taking them apart and assembling new words from those parts. A syllabic method would be the opposite: it departs from syllables and arrives at words. The phonetic method, which seeks to transform the articulation of sounds into a conscious process – this at least was something that I found interesting. But all these methods – synthetic, analytic, word-based, syllabic, even mixed methods – still just seemed so many words in and of themselves....

The disastrous over-simplification of these methods by well-meaning primary school teachers means that they end up being complicit in modes of literacy that are by turns mechanical, repetitive, alienating, stereotyping and so on. By virtue of its very design, any method will always be both precarious and insufficient to (the subject of) its task, which results in its furnishing literacy teachers with worksheets, labels, [pictures of] cute little animals, letters and frameworks that can only crush the child's capacity for creativity. But these methods remain the dominant means for teaching literacy, with no alternative. To my mind, the means must be determined by each individual group, every separate class. The method should not crush anyone.

One important contribution to the scholarship on child literacy has been made by Paulo Freire and his followers – the 'Freire method', if you like. This method has its own philosophy. Which is to say, literacy can only be understood as a means of rescaling the individual's whole humanity.

The search for 'generative words'[9] in Freire's work calls to mind the natural method of literacy education. It seems to me, however, that this method requires a particular level of consciousness of the learner, and always acts according to that level. As such, the Freirean method seems to me an excellent way of working with factory workers and farm labourers – people, that is, who already hold some sway over their own actions, who already understand themselves *as* people and can see the method for the political and revolutionary process that it is. In terms of an approach to literacy for the *favelados* (at least those without a strong political identity or affiliation), or for children, I think the method is limited. Work in this area cannot limit itself to conscious processes. It has to look deeper into the unconscious lives of individuals, the collective unconscious, the social imaginary....

Each person must be understood as a whole. We have to look closely at each person's modes of representation and self-representation, which are sought deep within their being. We need to look closely at their many languages.

And in terms of methods – well, I think we should always treat them with some suspicion. It would be better if we saw them for what they are: disposable objects that you use once and then throw away. What is the point of a method in-itself? The important thing is to create a method for every experience. It should be like the kind of risk taken in needlework that becomes its very own form of embroidery. Because with the birth of any method is the birth of a new form of domination. Any method, *a priori*, dampens the spirit of discovery.

I omitted to mention that at the beginning of every class there was a roll-call – not one of the conventional ones where the teacher simply checks that everyone is present. In this roll-call, it was the students who had to say the names of all their peers and be greeted by them.

The lack of personal identity amongst these kids was obvious. Besides not knowing each other's names, they had no idea of their own dates of birth, and the majority had no photos of themselves (I had asked them to bring in a family photo. Few of them brought one, and those that did asked their friends if they could identify which one was them, in amongst the rest

---

[9] Generative words, introduced in Freire's *Pedagogy of the Oppressed*, are the words used by people to name their world.

of the family). Some of my pupils had never seen themselves in a mirror, either because they had no mirror at home, or because they were afraid of becoming vain. The way they addressed each other also spoke to their lack of personal identity: they called each other by crude nicknames, such as Ugly Bug, One-Eye, Darky.

The celebration of Jussara's birthday must have been a special occasion for her. She brought a cake as promised, and the others brought in soft drinks. We divided the labour amongst us so there'd be no argument: some laid the table, others served the food and drink, others tidied the room. We all sang Happy Birthday and gave Jussara a big hug, then sat down for cake and soda.

It goes without saying that these celebrations took place at the *end* of the day's lessons. But I remember that during the class some of the kids had already begun to complain. Ana Paula, for example, had said '*Tio*, this class just isn't going anywhere. We're only coming to school to mess about. My dad is not happy about it'.

'Yeah, same here, *tio*!' said Celso. 'If we're going to pass the year, we need to be doing homework, exercises, copying things out. Play time is over.'

'But are you enjoying it?' I asked. 'Well, there you go then. Maybe I know what I'm doing after all. Do you not think that there's something different about the games we play?'

The days that followed Jussara's birthday brought with them some great discoveries....

I had been doing some reading around various subjects – Chinese characters, the art of Paul Klee, graphic arts in general – and it had got me thinking about the simplest forms of mark-making and representation. I sensed that this should be my departure point for getting through to the kids. In flicking through books on both ancient and modern China, I came across the *I Ching*, the Chinese book of divination, which is still in use today as a mode of telling the future. The *I Ching* functions as a kind of game in which fortunes are told by reading sequences of straight lines – either complete or broken in two – which are organized into sixty-four potential combinations of lines, known as 'hexagrams'. Each hexagram has its own meaning. For example, hexagram 48 is 'The Well':

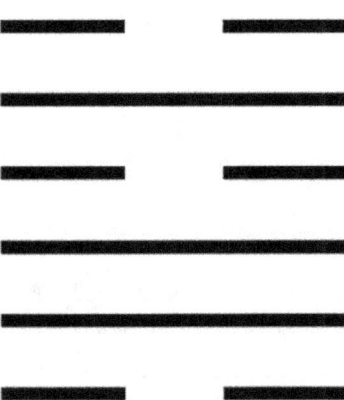

The ancients say that the hexagrams originated as the markings on turtle shells, from which the very first readings of the oracle were drawn.

It wasn't so much this mythical dimension of the *I Ching* that made me want to take it up with the kids as a kind of 'textbook' (though that is certainly worth exploring), but the graphic and textual potentialities of working with just two very simple lines: one stretched out, the other interrupted. I could envision beginning with the hexagrams themselves, and then working with them as the building blocks for images, then symbols and finally letters.

The path towards a new game of graphics lay open. What's more, I was beginning to get to know my students a little better by now, and I sensed a need to work both on their reclamation of identity as well as their group cohesion. We would have to entirely reconstruct the life-space in which they had been operating. This simple graphic game appeared to make that a possibility also.

The four hours I spent with the kids each day were enough to wear me out. I had so many expectations, very few skills and the class was admittedly chaotic. Every time I arrived home, I would debrief to my wife on the day's events in the classroom. Our lives in the year of 1981 were wonderful: she was writing alongside me, we split the housework between us, we'd spend ages talking about Rocinha's various issues, and plan the arrival of our first child, who was going to be born at home. Everything together.

Time flies with so much going on. Either you have to grab the moment with both hands, or watch it quickly slip through your grasp. Sometimes, if you don't make the very most of an opportunity handed to you, it becomes a difficulty instead.

Every time I came up with a lesson plan that had been carefully thought through, and failed to put it into action exactly as it was, I felt frustrated. It's always a much better idea to go into a classroom situation knowing that any judgment as to whether the plan should be used or not, can be made by taking the pulse of the classroom first. New discoveries always arise outside of what has been planned for in advance.

The day that I first presented the class with the *I Ching* hexagrams, I placed them into their simplest form. I gave each child a drawing book, and drew three hexagrams on the blackboard for them to then copy.

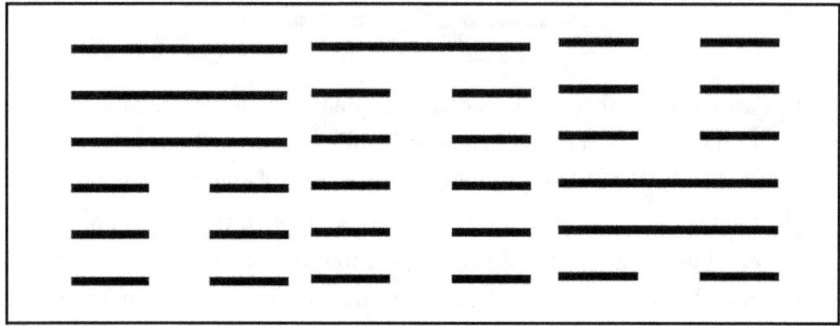

It was only once I'd done this that I realized I could have presented the hexagrams in a much more creative way. I could have put them on an acetate sheet, for example, and shown them on the projector. I could even have taken a turtle shell into the classroom and surprised the students with something so unusual that it would sanctify that very first impression. The traces, those first lines, would have appeared to them on the turtle's back…

I thought about all this just as I was finishing drawing the lines up in chalk on the board – those instruments of banality!

It seems to me that people first begin to write when they take up the pencil and carve into the page. Long before the written word, humans were already making decorative marks, ritual codes, etc. Humans had to first be writers before they could become clerks or scribes. First comes the mark *from inside*, the writing that sits closest to creation. Then comes the copy, the register, that script which attempts to fix the evanescence of the spoken word. The initial act of creation is to take note of that which had never before been said, it is the page of the mystic, of the healer, of the cabal, of esotericism….

On that very same day, as I was introducing the students to writing in a more organized way – albeit in unceremonious fashion – something quite unexpected occurred.

As the kids copied out their hexagrams, I found myself suddenly saying: 'Today you are starting to write! It's a new life!' And when they'd finished, I added that they'd no longer need their lined notebooks, nor any kind of book, or anything else, except the plain drawing book that I had given them.

'Now we're starting to write. Get your books out of your folders. Here are some scissors...'

We all sat in a circle. I sent for an enormous trash can, and it was placed in the middle of the room.

'And now I want you to cut out all the words from your books and primers, and throw them into the trash.'

They didn't ask why we were doing this. Perhaps they understood. The desecration of the primers was absolutely necessary.

'And now, *tio*?', asked Ana Paula, towards the end of the class.

'And now, my child, we are going to start making our own primers, using our own hands, from here until the end of the year.'

In March, I held a meeting for all the parents. I also attended another meeting for all the literacy teachers at the school, and then I was invited to participate in a series of further meetings in the school district, set up by the Secretary of State for Education's Special Education Advisory Panel.

The meeting for parents and guardians had an attendance of about 50 per cent. Instead of inviting them to come to the school separately, I had resolved to go to the house of each of the pupils, and to take a picture of them with their family. In so doing, I could take the opportunity to fill them in on the details of the meeting. On reflection, I think that I could have gone about this differently, or better. Instead of photographing the families myself, for instance, it would have been better for the kids to have done it themselves. Nevertheless, the day before paying them a visit, I did at least show them how a camera worked.

'The light writes our image down onto the film when we take a photo', I said.

For me, to offer this explanation was a matter of principle: any language that was presented to them, before they were shown its end product, they had to know how that language *worked*, how it is made. Every individual is possessed of the mechanisms for mastering a language. But languages reside in the emotions of individuals. Children must learn the mechanics of photography before they are exposed to photos. They should know how films are made before they encounter cinema. Their understanding of literature has to emerge from an awareness of words. Otherwise, the very media that ought to offer them their freedom, risk being the source of their oppression.

But why photograph the children in the first place? I thought it important that they know their own image, that they could familiarize themselves with their own faces, as a way of assuming their identity. Yes, I exist because I am engaged in my own self-creation.

At the meeting that I held with the parents, it was clear by their faces that they were somewhat disillusioned with their children's education. For the most part, they were migrants of little literacy and great suffering. Many of them had spent years going round hospitals in the belief that their child was fundamentally wrong in the head, that they were suffering from some kind of mental deficiency. In almost every case, they laid the blame for any mistakes in the child's education on the children themselves – not on the school.

From what I could observe, only two or three of my students might possibly have some kind of neurological disorder. After all, don't we all suffer from some form of dysrhythmia?

'The problems that your children are experiencing are not for hospitals to fix. The difficulties they are having, you are having also. Put simply, poor people don't have a right to a family, to a decent job with a living wage, or even a decent education. Eighty per cent of poorer people have no access to a school, and therefore they don't learn, just like your children….'

That evening I heard many a story about each child and about their families, told by their own parents. We talked about physical disciplining, smacking kids and the question of literacy. At the end of the meeting, I invited them to follow their child's progress with the drawing book. I told them that they could also write in the books what they wanted to. If they wanted to draw, they could draw. And at the end of every month, we would get together again, at least just to chat about what had been going on with the kids' work. (But for those parents who couldn't read, wasn't there a chance they could learn something along with their children?)

Family

'Poor people don't have the right to a family … '

Weddings are always happy occasions, and in the home of a poor person there is always at least a *feijoada*, some cachaça and beer on a day of celebration.

But the party doesn't last long: soon comes the first and then the second child, the beginning of a long line.

Generally speaking, the wife doesn't have a job at the beginning of a marriage: 'I want my wife at home to take care of the kids', the man will say.

And of course, it then turns out that he can't earn enough to sustain the entire family. The first row happens, and inevitably the wife wins: she ends up heading out to work also, to work in the homes of rich people, to make ends meet. Sometimes she works as a housemaid. When she goes out, she leaves her child with a trusty neighbour. But even then, the money is not sufficient. When the second child arrives, the difficulties mount up. Because the favela man is always doing casual labour, he is easily fired. This is a life both difficult and precipitous. The men find the precariousness of their labour difficult to understand, and they are not equipped with the intellectual means to fight back. So they start to drink, and they begin to develop a profound distaste for life itself. Soon, the men only return home to hit their wives and get them pregnant.

And they don't always return. Fights between husband and wife are the most commonly reported incidents recorded with the Rocinha Police Department.

So how then do we explain the fact that there are such a large number of children if the parents neither want them nor can support them? This kind of phenomenon can only be explained at the level of the unconscious: it is necessary to have a greater number of children to shore up against the suffering perpetrated by society towards the oppressed. This is simple survival of the species.

In all of this, the man takes no ownership of his actions. So, by the third or fourth child, he frequently abandons the home and the woman is left with the kids, who must then assume the task of taking care of one another whilst their mother goes to work. A five-year-old is already ready to make rice for her younger siblings. And she'll go and fetch water, far from home, sometimes returning late into the night. This could be a portrait of most of my students: no father, a mother working in service away from home. A portrait of abuse, and one in which children are left semi-abandoned, taking care of themselves and their domestic chores, entirely under the radar.

Before I discuss the meetings held with the school's other literacy teachers, or the meetings organized by the Special Education Advisory Board, let's return to Class 111.

We were pressing ahead with my graphic game. All of the students were capable of recognizing the differences between the hexagrams, making them bigger or smaller in size, and of either copying them or creating new ones. Now, at the beginning of every class, for whatever exercise we happened to be working on, we would put a small hexagram in the corner of the page. The hexagrams could be laid out on the page however the kids wanted.

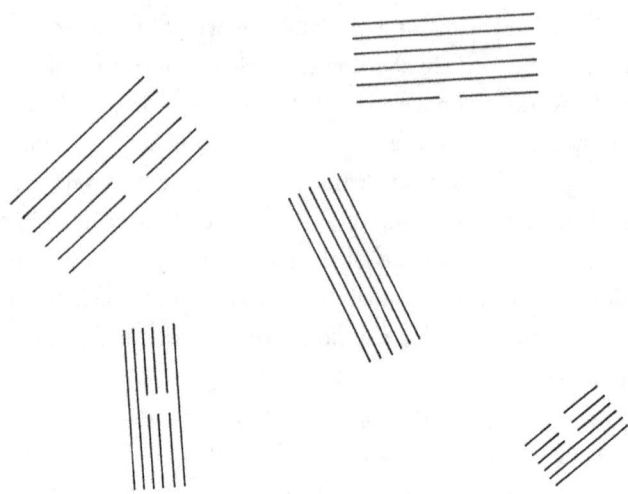

Having unburdened ourselves of the weight of all the material that the kids had been carrying around in their folders for years, something new now seemed to be happening. And these little hexagrams were a symbolic manifestation of that change: our very first sign, and one that we would hold on to.

Now we could go about looking for new signs, using both the long and short lines as a base, drawn faintly onto the page. By drawing over parts of the other lines, the new signs started to emerge:

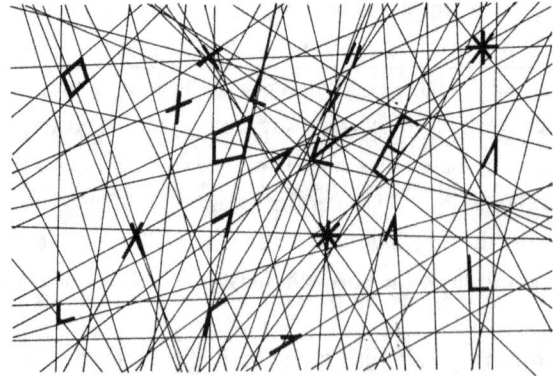

I then asked the kids to copy those new signs onto a sheet of blank paper:

Whilst we were working on this, I had the idea of giving a sound to each of the two lines in the hexagram: a long sound for the long line, and two short sounds for the broken line. I asked Márcio to get his drum, and we 'read' our first hexagrams in tune with the beat of the drum.

We then went through them again, reading the hexagrams whilst clapping hands: one clap for the long line, two short claps for the broken line.

And that was how my students began to read, and how we began to do dictation. The graphic games became sonic games. And we began to build games around the clapping system: we decided that the word 'fire', for example, would be represented by three short claps followed by three long ones. One group would clap and the other had to work out what was being said. The kids themselves devised their own games around the clapping system ... .

All of this may seem so trivial that it is unworthy of the reader's time. But I must admit that I found even the most trivial of discoveries to be fascinating.

Later on, I would figure out how to move from the line to the letter, and from the rhythm to the phonetically structured sound.

But let's go back a moment, to the Paula Brito literacy teachers' meeting.

Before we'd even begun, my colleagues were asking what I was doing at the meeting, given that I was a teacher of class with Special Educational Needs, and it didn't therefore make much sense for me to be participating in discussions with teachers of the 'normal' classes (you can see just how much an SEN teacher might feel marginalized within their own institution).

Moving on: I soon found out that the teachers at the school were really pretty unhappy in their work, and that they were, for the most part, people who were concerned with doing a good job. Paula Brito was one of the schools taking part in the Schools Support project developed by the Secretary of Education, which in 1980 had seen work begin on an 'Artistic Education' initiative that would involve most of the first-grade classes. This initiative had proven confusing for the teachers; to my mind, they just didn't see exactly what this change should involve or entail. Most were only ever looking for recipe-classes, tried-and-tested methods that would bring about the kinds of change that those recipes and methods required. It seemed to me that it was the teachers whose mindset needed changing – they would have to abandon their primers, their formulae, and in particular their authoritarian and overly maternal way with the children. Of course, this isn't something that changes with the wave of a magic wand. But all sorts of developments would and did happen over the course of 1981. I suggested, at our very first meeting, that the group put together a list of discussion points that would be addressed at every meeting, and that we meet on a regular basis – every week, on a Monday. If memory serves me correctly, our first lot of discussion points would be: recounting our own experience, creative education, discipline and pedagogical methods.

It is my belief that in order to be a teacher you can't only be focused on the lesson in front of you, but on the running, organization and the decision-making processes of the school as a whole. I also believe that a teacher has to get to know their own community, to seek out connections with the community teacher,[10]

---

[10] An individual whose job is to establish and affirm closer ties between school and local community.

with other individuals who are engaged in local cultural activities, and with the Residents Association. These are the outside forces that must have an impact on the school, and not the superstructural reforms.

'Vivo-Morto, Morto-Vivo' is a game from which you can develop many variations.

I always begin with the game itself. But then, you can ask people to close their eyes, relax, and begin making the Vivo-Morto, Morto-Vivo movements once more, but this time ever so slowly and imperceptibly, almost like the hands of a clock.

I remember one experience of playing Vivo-Morto with class 111. I had suggested to them that we begin in 'Dead' position, in a place where there isn't yet life – it was a kind of foetal position, but standing, with floppy arms and heads between legs. We should try and hear our hearts beating, I said, and make shoulder motions as if we were swimming in some form of liquid, being born slowly, passing from death to life, with our eyes closed. When we arrived at the standing position, the point of life, we should fill our lungs with air and release the loudest shout we possibly could, opening our eyes.

Alexandre Alves didn't just shout – he ran towards the cupboards and old doors that were out on the patio, pounding on them furiously, as if he were blindfolded. Then I asked him to repeat everything that he had just done, but in slow motion....

Intra-uterine injury, birth traumas, conception denial on the part of the mother, unskilled medics and mishandling at the time of birth – a vast range of birth-related problems – almost all of the kids in this class had been through it. The battle of life against death, from the very first moments: Alive-Dead, Dead-Alive.

I wanted to make them aware that the battle to be born was still alive in them.

We have to keep being born, to keep building our identities.

On to the next game: I had everyone sit in circles, with each one getting up in turn with their eyes shut and walking into the middle of the circle. Then I gave them the signal to stop. And just as they stopped, we would all shout out their name together: only then could the child open their eyes.

Another exercise: this time, each child would be stopped inside the circle with their eyes open. Each of their colleagues would offer one word about the person in the middle. The child comes to learn something about themselves through the eyes of others....

Games took up one part of the class. And now I was also introducing dictation, reading out loud, sign – discovery,[11] etc.

It was during one of my sign-discovery exercises that I realized something else that should have been obvious all along, right in front of my eyes: some of the children, whilst looking for signs in amongst the criss-crossed lines that we had been making, were actually coming across letters that they definitely recognized, and not just abstract signs. But the letters they were finding were, of course, rectilinear letters. And almost all these rectilinear letters were capitalized, and of a stick-like character, with a very simple shape. These were by no means representative of the difficulties involved in reading cursive or hand-written script. I suggested, therefore, that the kids look for letters hidden in amongst the lines, and this is what they came up with:

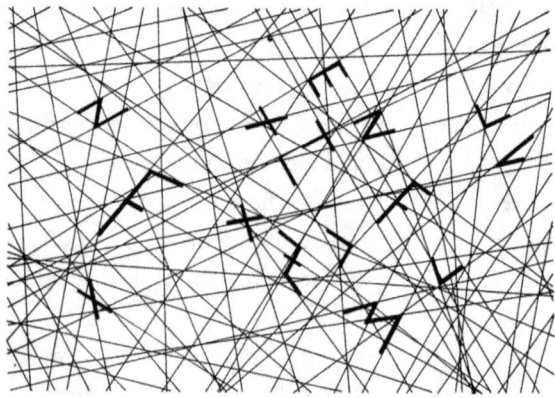

Although I knew that I wanted to get to working with capitalized rectilinear letters eventually, I felt that it was too soon to be trying to connect letters at this stage. Words aren't quite like sticks; they are drawn from the air. I would have to play more games. In particular, we would need to work more with our hands, because it is hands that create words, whether they are spoken or written.

Special education

Many years ago, when I first heard that there were students designated as 'SE' (Special Students), I admittedly thought that these must be students with some form of mental deficiency. My time with the kids at Paula Brito taught me that

---

[11] That is the game of crossed lines, amongst which the children had to identify signs, as illustrated above.

this kind of student, now referred to as having Special Educational Needs, is something altogether different. I prefer to call them marginalized students. These are kids who, despite sometimes having no family or only a very fragile familiar framework, have become part of the favela's habitat, however chaotic it might be. They have experienced disease and hunger, and could thus be seen as symptomatic of a broader social malaise; but they also have their networks of support, and a tremendous instinct for survival. These kids aren't 'deficient', 'parasitic' or 'irrelevant', at least not from the point of view of their community. It's only the current system that views them as such, a system that has to create an idea of the abnormal simply to justify its own laws, injustices and the apparatus of police and military. It is the system that contrives marginality by means of its own institutions. It has to first label people as marginal to then legitimize their maltreatment.

If I speak here *not* of the 'Special Student', but of the marginalized student, it is because the schooling system, the pulpit of a State that is invested in the creation of states of marginality, is also responsible for the marginalization of kids that seek an education within it. To put it more bluntly: the school is the very first institution to put into effect the marginalization of the Favela child. Schools have their methods and their curricula for instigating that exclusion from the get-go. The wheat is to be promptly separated from the chaff; a wall is immediately built between those who are normal and those who are marginal. Between those that can't face the challenge of that wall, and those that find themselves defeated after First Grade, almost 80 per cent of students drop out of school... or, in some form or another, they are asked to leave. Of course, with this first defeat come others. These young people will soon find themselves with no identity card, no personal documentation, no basic entitlements under the law. And once they find themselves thus outside of the law, they will soon encounter further marginalization from other institutions, not least the all-powerful beast that is our combined judicial, police and military system.

Because education is in principle both free and compulsory for all Brazilians between the ages of seven and fourteen, according to the constitution, the school also violates the law by marginalizing thousands of young Brazilians, which is to say: the school is complicit in unconstitutionality.

By way of dealing with all these marginalized students, the Ministry of Education has set up an advisory committee on Special Education, along with its own Institute: The Helena Antipoff Institute.

The points I am about to make do not relate to every aspect of the functioning of either the advisory panel or the Institute. But what I want to focus on here is the precise relation that exists between the bureaucratic-political-administrative superstructure, and every individual teacher of a Special Education class.

The first problem this relationship encounters is the verticality of the administrative process within the Ministry, whereby decisions are taken top-downwards with absolutely no intermediary. Neither at the level of the Department for Education and Culture, nor at school level, are people entitled to an opinion on Special Education. The teachers themselves are mere executors of orders that come direct from the Ministry, whilst also being seen as outsiders within their own school community.

At the series of meetings which I was invited to sit in on as part of my training to become a Special Education literacy teacher, this was the format: six small handouts from the advisory committee were distributed amongst the teachers present, and the teachers would then be instructed in the use of a single methodological approach and in the criteria for its propagation, observing the pre-determined stages for a single word-based method.

I disagreed with both the method and its mode of evaluation, and said that, for my part, I would be seeking out other avenues, based on what I had learned from my activities already. I began to speak of what I thought I had discovered until that point and of my need to exchange experiences with others, because my understanding was that these meetings ought to be about such exchanges.

I was informed that there was no such thing as a 'special student' – a term which provided the perfect excuse for not confronting the marginalization of certain students – but that there was a special *method*, which was proposed by the advisory committee. I thought this both absurd and arbitrary. This committee was not only dealing with a vast number of kids, but it didn't want to know anything about the sorts of learning challenges those kids were facing. It simply wanted to put forward a *method*, a term with a curiously orthopaedic, mechanical ring to it. This committee had no interest in the reality of any of the students, simply the application of its method.

The simple fact of having one teacher's voice raised against this procedure brought the issue to the committee's attention, and the answer came back immediately. If I chose not to adhere to the method, I would no longer be in charge of a Special Education class, and I would receive no further support or supervision. In sum: they simply wanted to ignore any new ideas, any search for alternatives.

As a result, I ended up writing, in October of that year, a letter to the *Jornal do Brasil*, with the title 'An impaired education'. It was published in full on the 17th of November:

In this, the International Year of the Physically Impaired, our schools will produce once again a sad annual spectacle: the departure from their desks of thousands upon thousands of children, some of whom are ill-equipped, delinquent, unprepared, and others who are just plain naïve and rebellious.

Confronted with a cultural apparatus and with [teaching] methods that treat them with little dignity, school becomes the place in which these children first experience defeat in life, an experience from which it is difficult to recover: they cannot become literate.

There is a generalized crisis in our system of education, but it is literacy that sits at the epicenter: amongst the *lumpenproletariat*, statistics of dropout and failure in the first year of Elementary School stand at 80%. And the system has no idea how to solve this problem.

As a High School teacher in Rio de Janeiro, I have experienced the joy of trying out a number of new, forward-thinking educational activities with students, that draw freely on different languages (cinema, theatre, the written word), and as a result I have always been intrigued by the current state of our literacy and its constraints.

But it was in March of this year that I finally rolled my sleeves up and entered the fray, taking on the task of teaching literacy to a Special Education class (students who have been in their first year of Elementary for more than three years without learning basic literacy skills) at the Paula Brito School, in Rocinha. It has been the greatest experience of my life as an educator. This letter aims to inform the readers of the *Jornal do Brasil* of the actions of the Advisory Committee on Special Education at the Helena Antipoff Institute – which is to say, the body with principal oversight for this part of the education system.

Shortly after the beginning of March, I was invited to take part in a series of meetings with a group of people connected to the Helena Antipoff Institute with responsibility for Special Education delivery. Everything about these meetings conformed to the usual bureaucratic regimen: the paperwork – in the form of six small handouts – was distributed amongst the teachers by the team's three psychologists. I studied the handouts and immediately took issue with the approach being proposed by the committee: the idea was that there would be a single approach (word-based) for the entire District; the approach was intended to effect control over the students; it entirely underestimated the teachers' own creative capabilities, training them instead in the exercise of filling out forms with little meaning to them; it entailed a vertical line of authority that ran directly from the Ministry of Education right down to the student, taking no account of the particularities of school, teacher, or individual student, beyond their being seen as an object of measurement and not individuals in their own right; it treated individual student needs under the general categories of 'Special' – which is to say, there is no such thing as this 'maladjusted' child, or that child with 'learning difficulties', there is only a method for kids objectively categorized according to these terms. I quote: 'There is no child classified as having special educational needs; Special Education refers only to the mode of attendance, i.e., attendance at Special Education classes'. This kind of wording, in my view, does much to mask the real problem, and to make of the method one that is dangerously one-size-fits-all. But my list could go on. The first column of one handout titled 'Student Performance Record Sheet' reads as follows: 'If you observe the student reading up to four words of basic visual vocabulary, make a note of this development in their assessment books using the brown pencil…'. At this point, our instructor – poor thing – then asked: 'And has everyone found the colored pencils we'll need to learn how to fill out our forms?'. It was that bad…

But let's move on. When I said that I disagreed with this approach, and that I would be looking for another, I was suddenly informed on the 18th May of that year that my class would no longer be classified as Special Education. In short, from that day onwards my students would cease to be thought of as misfits. Finally, thank God! In truth, I recognize that this was the system's subtle mode of sidelining my work and thereby not having to engage in internal discussions about my methods. During the International Conference on Special Education, when the Heads of the Committee were supposed to be strutting their stuff at the Hotel Nacional, I received another message: 'We'd like to hear your ideas about class 111, Mr Leal'. So I replied: 'But my class is no longer classified Special Education!'. They came back to me with a clever twisting of their own words: 'Perhaps not in a methodological sense, but they will continue to be understood as such statistically speaking…'. Quite the merry-go-round, isn't it?

Behind all these observations that might pass for mere anecdote, there lies a distinct ideological agenda: totalitarianism, authoritarianism, and control, without doubt inspired by some American Skinner-type psychology. And this is how special education is being treated in our city.

Now is the time to get together: teachers, parents, neighborhood associations – we need to get together in search of alternatives to this primitive pedagogy for the majority population. When the system cannot prevent an 80% dropout in the first grade, it is not the students who have been found wanting. It is the system.

Just a few more brief words about Special Education: students who currently fall under the purview of the Advisory Committee on Special Education constitute a minority within favela-based schools. The 'normal' children make up a much larger part of their population. But what I would come to perceive in time was that entire classes of these 'normal' kids were also being condemned. I have realized that special attention should not just be reserved for those who have been designated as 'special', but extended to the entire 80% of those pupils who are failing through being failed – those that drop out, those that have to repeat, and those who refuse to attend. In short, the favelas *demand* their own special education, one that is right for their children. The greater the oppression, the greater should be our effort to do right by the oppressed: smaller classes, specialist teacher training, the use of lay members of staff, adequate equipment, etc. – herein lies what should be special about our approach to education. But can a State that oppresses and marginalizes be persuaded to take an interest in justice for the marginalized and oppressed?

Babies spend a long time looking at their own hands. Human hands seem to transcend their motor function. The baby's study of its own hands attests to their complexity: more than just the limbs of an animal, these are the tools we use to transform the world of things. It is the hands that have shaped the human mind and its entire culture.

I played countless games with the kids, with the aim of exploring the use of their hands, to the point of unhardening them, making them instead supple and warm, preparing them for care and affection… We have to keep going back to the hands as our tools for mark-making, grasping and building in the construction of our labour and our existence.

Our point of departure is always game-playing… The child's game of 'Pass the Ring'[12] might be a good opener. This game allows the kids to:

Examine closely their own hands
Examine the hands of others closely
Feel the touch of another
Recognize the hands of each of their classmates
Conduct group exercises, with eyes closed, where they have to seek out the hands of classmates,
Create panels with the outlines of hands and feet of each child in the class
Express feelings – affection, hate – and actions using just the hands, in a number of different exercises: writing, gardening, greeting, punching, etc.

Handprints, fingerprints – an alphabet all of their own – allow us to read someone's hand. Hands and their contours must have something to do with the writing that they themselves create, maybe even the fact that they look so alike.

---

[12] A game in which one child holds a ring between cupped hands, and goes round the circle of children passing their hands between the others' cupped hands, until at some point they drop the ring surreptitiously into the hands of another. The child dropping the ring gets to choose another child to guess where it is.

The hands of my students are hardened hands, they are unsure, nervous, sweaty, hidden, cold, abandoned, marked by scars big and small. But they are hands that are moved at the first caring touch … .

All the work that we had begun to do using the two primordial lines – first abstractly with the pencil, then in more concrete fashion using matchsticks, pasta or string – were about circumscribing aspects of life. Only straight lines, for instance, could be used to show a face:

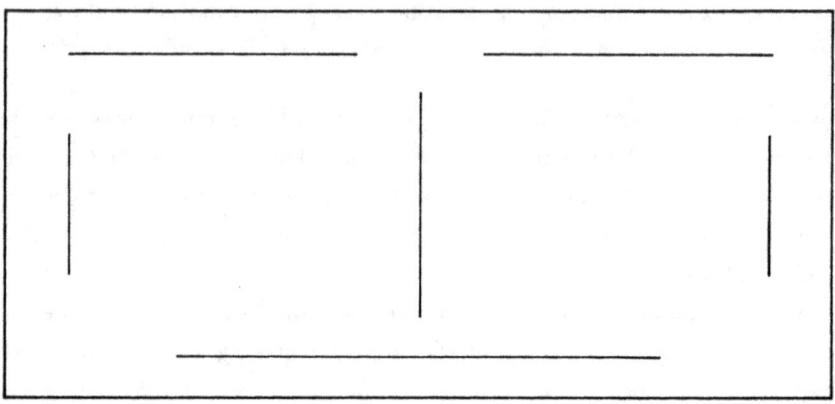

Using these tools, we went on to build ourselves houses, to build ourselves favelas:

One boy, Carlos Alberto, captivated me with his designs, with the way he used the lines… He wasn't so much playing with the meaning of things, but with everything as meaningful… Carlos Alberto was an artist. I'll come back to this kid later on.

We had taken the primordial lines as far as they could go. I'm not sure how, but one day I made another discovery. Perhaps it was as a result of Márcio's drumming. Márcio wasn't interested in the written lines on the board, or those in his classmates' books. To tell the truth, very little interested him, even the game-playing. José Edmilson was just about enough of a friend for his monosyllabic personality. The rest of the time he would spend drumming his own soliloquy out on his desk. But I then remembered that he had his own actual drum.

When I decided to allocate the long line in any hexagram one long sound, and the broken line two short sounds, and beat these out on the drum, I was rewarded in two ways: I opened up the association between line and sound, thereby overcoming its coded appearance; and from this point, Márcio – who previously hadn't been coming to school very often – began to take an interest, to attend more and take part in the classes.

But Márcio's role didn't end simply with his appearance in class. I asked him to get his drum out again. 'Márcio, please read with your drum what is shown on the board', I said.

```
————      —  —      ————
————      ————      —  —
—  —      —  —      ————
————      ————      —  —
—  —      ————      —  —
————      —  —      ————
```

And he read.
I then asked everyone else to read the sounds with their hands, clapping along...
'Now', I said, 'Let's read with our mouths'
'How, sir?' They asked.
'Use your mouths to read...'
'I don't get it...'
'OK, what does a heartbeat sound like?'
'I know', said Alexandre Gomes. 'TA, TA – TA, TA'
'Great – now read this out loud'
I went to the board, and drew below the hexagrams:

```
                TA              TA              TA
         TA   TA           TA   TA              TA
         TA   TA              TA                TA
              TA              TA   TA        TA   TA
         TA   TA              TA                TA
              TA              TA                TA
```

I had found a way to link the line, not with a free and ever-changing sound, but to a phonetically structured sound mass.

This noise was the sound equivalent of our primordial lines, potentially akin to the first sounds made by primitive humans. And it is also amongst the first sounds made by babies when they first begin to babble.

As this latest finding unfolded, I noticed a significant number of coincidences.

The student

The favela child is active, creative by nature, and lively. When confronted with an all-knowing educator, who belongs to a different social class and tries to mould the child according to the image of the more dominant class, the favela child becomes a mere passive observer and listener. When going to school, the favela child has to leave their world on the outside and adopt different manners and customs.

The process of a child becoming a fully realized *student* is one in which she must become obedient and observe the rules for behaviour set out by the school. The bad student, by default, is the one that does not submit to the school's brainwashing, who instead of adapting rebels and deliberately messes up. But this messing up should really be understood as critique of, or reaction to, the level of understanding about these children. Kids growing up in favelas are usually bad students: they are critics, they mess things up, they rebel.

A child has to be the subject of their own self-transformation, and not some blueprint apathetic-student-object. They should be allowed to bring their world into the school, with the aim of processing it there. Beyond this, it is vital that we all learn how to work *with* – and not against – messing up, with rebelling, with criticism and with violence.

Class 111 is no exception to the rule: it is a restless, mischievous, rebellious, critical and at times violent class. It could of course be different. I could run a quiet and well-ordered class, held in its place with rules or threats: the kids sit down, they shut their mouths, they repeat, they copy, I give them a zero, they are reprimanded, they follow the textbook, etc.

But if the teacher is willing to listen, as I was, and to really hear the students, to hear their music, their games, their stories – their culture, in fact – and goes further, freeing them, removing the censure placed on them such that their unconscious and their imagination is allowed free voice, it is possible that any class of nice young children could rapidly turn into a very troubling class. Which is to say, a liberated classroom might well be a troubling classroom, because it becomes fertile ground for discovery and for creativity.

Of course, such ideas have their extremes. Even when the school rules are abandoned, new rules will find their way to being established, generally by the class itself. Class 111 was a noisy class, in which all the kids wanted to speak at the same time. So they would then proceed to tell each other off, becoming irritated at the noise they themselves were making. At this point, we would pause whichever activity was going on to talk about issues like excessive noise, the arguments between the students, and the nature of violence.

A lot of the time I was exhausted. The four hours each day I spent with 111 tired me out more than eight hours of manual labour.

The teacher, creative as they may be, won't always have ideas to hand for when the students are no longer satisfied with the activity they are doing. We would try and divide our time between more active and more relaxing exercises, between dramatic games and written ones, as part of the routine. The thing I found most difficult was ensuring that the exercises going on in the class were sufficiently diverse, engaging in various activities at the same time.

The main reason behind the generalized indiscipline on the part of any one student was usually down to a lack of understanding, engagement or immediate results that spoke to them directly. And any such failure in the work process can result in a child feeling marginalized within the overall dynamic of the class. The child sees others making progress and sees that they aren't making the same progress, and so they rebel, breaking the rules set down by the group left, right and centre. A teacher has to be on guard against these deviations, so that they can find new ways to pull the child back. Because no one should stop making progress as long as the processes are right for them. So if I wasn't making a lot of headway with Antônio Marcos, for example, it wasn't because he had stopped progressing, but because the processes that I had come up with were still not right for his needs.

The kids most lacking in discipline and adjustment were: Antônio Marcos, Clodoaldo, Alexandre Alves, Rivelino and Paulo José. They could become quite aggressive and often disrupted the general classroom flow. There were a handful of others who were more apathetic, who would either give up, fade out or withdraw over the course of any exercise, or would simply follow the task mechanically and obediently. One thing was completely clear and obvious to me: a lack of discipline never manifests for the sake of it – as a merely gratuitous act, or incurable ill, an innate spirit of provocation.

The drawing game, at least, was one which *all* the students had got the hang of, without exception. Antônio Marcos, whose writing was always back-to-front, had a few difficulties. But these exercises, even if they couldn't be specific enough to iron out each of their individual problems, were helping them to advance in the sense of experiencing a kind of pleasure in the adventure, and they no longer represented the frustratingly repressive schematics of formal approaches to reading and writing. The liberating gestures of game-playing seemed to be bringing the children together whilst giving each one a sense of their own personal development. Later, when I became more obsessive about the results of my alphabetization, the old frustrations returned, and those students who were being left behind, such as Antônio Marcos, began to feel marginalized once more, and became increasingly hostile.

We soon familiarized ourselves with the phonetically structured 'TA', which had emerged from our experiments with the primordial lines of the *I Ching*. The closest relative of this 'TA' sound, culturally speaking, seemed to me to be the sound 'LA'. Sambas and other songs all have a 'LA LA LA' to them, so their rhythms would form hooks and binds between the 'TA' and the 'LA'. We wrote:

	LA
	LA LA
	LA LA
	LA LA
	LA
	LA

For the time being we would only work with straight lines. The 'LA' began to reinforce the 'TA'. Two or three days after I'd introduced the new sound, I asked the children to bring some water buckets to school. They were tin cans of all shapes and sizes. Márcio brought his drum. We first drew a hexagram in one corner of the board. We then wrote out separate hexagrams for 'TA' and 'LA' sounds, like so:

TA	LA LA
TA	LA LA
TA	LA LA
TA TA	LA
TA TA	LA
TA TA	LA

We wrote out various hexagrams in this way, some that were 'read' just by clapping, others with the sound 'TA', others with the 'LA'. All of these were drawn up on the board by the kids themselves. In the meantime, I was allowing a bit of mystery to build up surrounding the tin cans.

'Sir, why have we brought these cans in with us, huh?' they asked.
'Yeah, what are the cans for?'
'To create a beat, man.'
'Well, let's make a beat then!'

Finally, I called Márcio over and asked him to set the rhythm with his drums. We all then chimed in on the beat with our tin cans and voices. After a period of high-energy beat-making, we decided to push the tables and chairs to one side, leaving a space in the middle of the classroom for us to sit on the floor with our tin cans. With eyes closed this time, we began to examine our cans, in their every detail: we registered their form, their volume, their smell, their temperature and their sound. We then did the same with each other's tin cans, still with our eyes closed, still taking note of the same details, comparing them with our own.

'You must try out everyone's cans and then stop only once you have found your own once more, without opening your eyes.'

They then sat looking at their own cans, but some of them quickly realized that there was something new written up on the board.

They looked at it with curiosity, until one of them said: 'Hey sir, doesn't what you've written up there say "CAN"?'

'It does, young man – how did you figure that one out? Let's try something. Hold your can against your chest and read what is written on the board.'

They then wanted to write the word in their books. A lot of them filled an entire page writing it out.

The word *can* ('lata')[13] is highly significant for people who live in the favelas. For many of my 111 students, it was evocative of hard work. When their parents were at their jobs, the children would often be the ones to take up the domestic chores: sweeping the house, making the food, doing the washing up, bathing their younger siblings, etc. But by far the hardest task, which all

---

[13] The word 'lata' most often refers to a standard tin can, but here evokes the kinds of jerrycan used to transport water from wells.

of them tried to avoid, whether adult or child, was carrying water. Often, kids will find themselves being dragged out of bed, either at night or early in the morning, to go with their parents or on their own to the well. These are anxiety-and-fear-inducing journeys into the dark of the night, through narrow, winding, steep and slippery streets. Balancing the can on their heads, in the hazy twilight, they will hear shootings, groans. They'll be afraid of the police and shotgun fire; in every starving dog they'll see a ghostly spirit or werewolf. For a small child with nothing but a bucket on their head, these are some remarkable odysseys!

One question that I often have cause to raise against Paulo Freire and other practitioners of a naturalist approach to literacy, has to do with their overemphasis on social realism and political realism. Written words aren't 'real' in any *a priori* sense. They are in fact abstract. Language can't as such be marshalled as an instrument to awaken a political conscience right away. It is so much more embedded than that, so much more reliant upon our expression of it, a much deeper and more complex expression. It is that depth from which we draw its political significance. 'LATA' is not an immediately *real* word; it is a simple combination of straight lines, but with a fantastical referent.

I proceeded to the sound 'FA':

```
                    FA
              FA         FA
              FA         FA
              FA         FA
                    FA
                    FA
```

And so it was that we discovered the word 'FALA' (speaks).
This latest step then prompted the phrase:

        A LATA FALA
        (The can speaks)

FA		TA		LA	
FA	FA	TA		LA	LA
FA	FA	TA	TA	LA	LA
FA		TA	TA	LA	LA
FA		TA	TA	LA	
FA		TA	TA	LA	

In terms of the creation of new words, the possible combinations of the sounds 'TA', 'LA' and 'FA' are relatively few. But in terms of basic sounds, phenomenal sounds and generative sounds, the potential for new meaning was enormous.

We picked up our cans again, laid down a cloth similar to those used for puppet shows, and transformed each of our cans into a puppet, that is, a talking being. It was incredible. It was quite amazing to see Clodoaldo's can-puppet speak. It was our first attempt at a puppet show, and we would return to it again.

Each can-puppet was then decorated with hexagrams, signs and letters, all in black and red, which were the colours of the class's magic marker.

This first spontaneous venture into representation led me to think about a possible dramatic thread that might run throughout the school year. We would have to devise a narrative core, beginning with the can-characters that had been born from our first improvised session. We already had a can-mother and can-child that had stood out most. We decided on a name for each and went with *Maria Favela* for the mother, and *Vavá* for the child. Aside from the names, which we hadn't yet written down, one important word had newly emerged – a word which might be fairly inconspicuous in the more gradual process of learning to read and write, but is of vast importance within the combined lives of the members of class 111. That word is *favela*. I said to the children, 'Read this':

FALA

I wrote the word down again, leaving a short space between the two sounds:

FA LA

Again, the kids read the word *fala*, and so now I wrote down the following:

FAVELA

And I asked: 'Who's going to read this one?' Marcelo read it straight off. I asked them to write the word down in their books. And then I added two further phrases:

A LATA FALA (*The can speaks*)
A FAVELA FALA (*The favela speaks*)

I was concerned to make sure we really fixed the sounds. In particular I wanted them to get the 'FA'.

We then sang a well-known song:

Comprei um quilo de farinha (*I bought a kilo of flour*)
FA ro FA FA[14]
etc.

I noticed that this song had a structure similar to some of our earlier activities, and so we used it to improvise new situations. I came up with the notion of reintroducing this tune whenever I wanted to bring something up for discussion with the class.

For example:

Comprei um quilo de farinha (*I bought a kilo of flour*)
FA ro FA FA
E um quilo de feijão (*And a kilo of beans*)

Alexandre ficou em casa (*Alexandre stayed at home*)
FA ro FA FA
E foi ver a confusão (*And went to see the fight*)

Quando menos esperava (*When he least expected*)
Fa ro FA FA
Ele levou um bofetão (*He was slapped*)

If Alexandre accepted the challenge, he would have to reply with a scenario of his own. The kids revelled in these challenges, and they really got them talking.

Sticking with our three basic words, few of the students could go wrong. So I pressed ahead, with the natural way forward seeming to be the 'MA' of *Maria*, even if the 'RI' of her name – much like the 'VE' of favela, would have to remain unknown for the time being. I couldn't dwell on this too much, and instead presented the new sound to them:

---

[14] Farofa is a traditional Brazilian side dish made with toasted cassava or corn flour mixture.

	MA	MA
	MA	MA
	MA	MA
	MA	MA
	MA	MA
	MA	MA

From here, it was only a short step to the words:

> MAMA (S/he suckles)
> AMA (S/he loves)
> MATA (Forest)[15]
> LAMA (Mud)
> FAMA (Fame)
> MARIA (Maria)

And from there we could form the phrases:

> A LATA TÁ NA FAVELA (The can is in the favela)
> A LATA FALA (The can speaks)
> A MATA TÁ NA FAVELA (The forest is in the favela)
> MARIA FAVELA FALA (Maria Favela speaks)
> MARIA FALA (Maria is speaking)

And finally:

FALA MARIA FAVELA.

Herein lies the origin of the title to this book, *Fala Maria Favela* (A Voice for Maria Favela). Doesn't cultural starvation lead to the death of a marginalized

---

[15] A number of the words used in this sequence have more than one meaning in Brazilian Portuguese, according to context. For instance, the word 'MATA' can be either a verb meaning 'S/he kills', or it is a noun that means 'wood(land)'. To avoid confusion, we have gone for the word which is consistent with its use in the rest of the text, but it is likely that the children would have been aware of the dual resonances of many of these words.

population's speech? Wasn't that what happened with the Amazonian Indians as a result of the Jesuit missions? But people from the favelas still speak. More than that, they conjure exorcisms, they whisper laments, they cry out in despair. At times, though, it is hard, things become complicated – you have to excuse the boy because it is the man who refuses to take up his language. But how can you alphabetize someone who doesn't have a voice? I have witnessed students with two, three, or four years of schooling and they still don't speak. Some of my students from class 111 were like that: almost entirely mute. And what do the teachers do when this happens? They continue teaching. But what exactly are you teaching, if you are teaching to people who can't speak? Truthfully, this very problem shows the clear extent to which school reproduces the repressive framework that prevents people from having a voice: the judgement, the abuse of power, the lack of respect for another, the physical abuse, authoritarian relations, the lack of an emotive frame of reference ...

Maria Favela is an immigrant who comes from Bahia. *Vavá* is her son. Maria has no husband, and she works as a housemaid. Vavá has never learned anything at school, and Maria is illiterate. This year, something about Vavá is changing: he is always asking questions as soon as Maria gets home. She answers them as best she can. But she is speaking to him. Vavá is bringing his school books home. He tells Maria that she must learn with him: 'The teacher says we shouldn't just be quiet!'

More meetings with the literacy teachers at the school. The person 'hosting' the meetings was always a supervisor, most of the time full of good intentions, but ultimately still an inexperienced and bureaucratic go-between. What might have been a kind of embryonic research group for literacy teachers, which already had a running theme for its meetings, which took its cue from the very concrete experiences of the teachers at Paula Prito, was beginning to lag. At one of these meetings there was an opportunity for me to talk about the various games I had been working on. We even tried a few out, did some exercises. But for the most part, the teachers were entirely indifferent. They remained silent. Some admitted to wanting some better-prepared tools, a prescription that would allow them to acquire the medicine for their sick pupils. A small minority showed some interest, including Elcy, the oldest and most lively member of the group. Elcy helped me a lot in my work. She offered me, and everyone else, a whole load of textbooks and other materials that I could use in the classroom.

But our discussions ultimately came to nothing. Which prompted me to think: where is the voice of the teacher in all this? Their *real* voice? These teachers simply remained mute. And, of course, they continued to give their same old classes which didn't speak to their students at all. And they had nothing to say to themselves. Change? For what? The immutable order of the world seemed beyond reversibility. And so our Monday meetings ceased to be.

Teaching

Teacher-student relations are established primarily through speech and writing. Teaching goals derived from these relations should not be based on the traditional rhetorical strategies of showing that the other side is lacking in knowledge, destroying the opponent's arguments, placing the teacher (as source of knowledge) in opposition to the student (as the one who knows nothing). Speech and writing must instead be treated as sacred, and as respected forms of expression for each and every individual.

Accordingly, the truth will be seen to reside less with particular individuals, than in the words of all the elements that make up any one group.

Teaching methods, as products of the pedagogical process, will also not exist outside of the needs of the group. They will be developed as objective requirements arise.

The teacher, then, should no longer have at his fingertips a set of methods or any other aid, which he relies upon *a priori* to teach better. The teacher should be deprived of such a weapon, since the students, in principle, do not possess it.

The most important thing in the classroom will no longer be the curriculum, the plan, the method; instead, the teacher's experience and 'training' should be grounded more in creative practices than in the repetition of method.

The teacher should always, when entering the classroom, say to himself: 'I know nothing'.

A priori methods and stimulus-response psychologies are all useless here – they are mendacious, and free no one. Does anyone believe in the value of an entrance exam? A new approach to teaching would be founded on creative practices, study practices and liberatory practices (political practices), in the games and play of local tradition. The new teacher-in-training would have to pass through theatre workshops, creative writing workshops, therapy work; he should get to know all kinds of work – from earth-based to machine-based, from the artisanal to the industrial – he must be familiar with political praxis, from classical to modern political literature, and the entire history of seizing power. In addition, he should get to know all the games and toys of local tradition, and learn how to develop other games from them. He should be very aware of the journeys that need to be taken from the unconscious to the conscious, from the imaginary to the political. But are trainee teachers aware of these things? Are any of us?

All this is said in the knowledge that this is a proposal for a new kind of teaching that can never be fully complete. Perhaps then it is not the way for teachers, but for true masters.

Besides the meetings with first grade teachers, I was invited to take part also in meetings of the 'Escola Sustentação' (School Support) project, in which the Paula Brito School was also involved. I felt that my participation in these meetings could be of use, given that my previous experience in the mainstream had taught me a lot about how schools might be improved.

A new kind of school cannot emerge without involving the community, or without embracing local culture. It was hard to see how these kinds of ideas could ever become objectives of the ['Escola Sustentação'] project, hence my scepticism towards top-down projects, which are always confused and full of jargon. But it was this project that initiated some of the formal discussions around the school-community relationship. These discussions, as with everything under the *Abertura Política*,[16] were still conducted very much under the watchful eye of the regime, *manu militari*. They say 'Discuss', and the people discuss; just as they used to say: 'Do not discuss', and the people obeyed. Both discussion and the *Abertura* still demanded a kind of obedience, the following of orders. Nevertheless, the discussions we had served to define and to deepen the word community in my own personal A to Z.

Community

The word 'community' on its own has virtually no meaning – is it a place, perhaps? Or could it be something more?

The concept of community today has nothing in common with primitive, tribal communities, which were more deeply entwined at the cultural and social level – like one organism. But when we speak nowadays of 'community work', it is almost to concede that the community no longer exists. In general, this work goes on in places termed 'communities-in-need', so that we can avoid creating

---

[16] Literally the 'political opening', the *Abertura Política* refers to the transitional period from military dictatorship to democracy in Brazil, a time of liberalization when a number of educational reforms were also implemented.

neologisms such as *incommunities, acommunities* or using synonyms for them such as *agglomerations* and *conglomerations*.

But is it the case that, despite everything, the people that inhabit these human amalgams – whether in the favelas or somewhere similar – will have forever lost their communitarian roots, their identity and their ability to relate to their own kind, however disparate their cultural origins may be?

It seems to me that if we are to reaffirm community ties, we shouldn't attempt to do so by trying to deepen their sense of origin. Which is to say, it wouldn't make sense to reconstruct the culture of the favela inhabitants according to the places from which they emigrated, nor according to some utopian ideal of a primitive community that fails to take into account the passing of time.

The favelas produce more by way of culture in a decade than some communities produce in millennia. This comes down to the fact of a *super*abundance of repressive mechanisms used by the State in the service of the dominant classes, which requires a corresponding *super*production of culture in those they oppress – armed with shields of resistance, adorned with the halo of life, the favelas produce a primordial cry for survival amongst the humiliated, the downtrodden, the barefooted, the *sans-culottes*. These are the true heroes of history, the people's real city-builders.[17]

The community of Rocinha, where I had been working for some time, was absorbing me bit by bit. I was getting to know people: the mothers of the students, the men and women who went every day to collect water from the well, people who worked with the Residents' Association, others who had become 'lay' teachers,[18] and were closely connected with a UNICEF development project in Rocinha. For me, community began with building these kinds of bridges.

The political sphere of my work, as I've already mentioned, began – but did not end – in the classroom. There were other overlapping spheres also: the meetings with other first-grade teachers, the meetings with the Support for Schools Project (and with others that would follow on from that, such as the Class Council project), the meetings with the DEC[19] and the contact that would need to be nurtured most of all: the Rocinha lay teachers.

---

[17] The phrasing in the original, 'esses construtores das verdadeiras cidades dos homens', is likely a latent reference both to another of Rio de Janeiro's neighbourhoods, the Cidade de Deus (City of God), and to Augustine of Hippo's fifth-century text, *City of God*.

[18] That is Teachers with qualifications in fields other than pedagogy/education.

[19] Departamento de Educação e Cultura (Department of Education and Culture)

Vavá was the name chosen by the kids as the name for *Maria Favela*'s son. VAVÁ was also a word that could be drawn in straight lines, so 'VA' was naturally the next sound to be worked on.

The sound 'VA' significantly increased our possible combinations of sounds. The kids were given the following words and phrases:

> LAVA (*S/HE WASHES*)
>
> VAVÁ (*MARIA FAVELA'S SON*)
> VALA (*DITCH*)
>
> VAVÁ MAMA (*VAVÁ SUCKLES*)
> VAVÁ AMA MARIA (*VAVÁ LOVES MARIA*)
> MARIA LAVA NA VALA (*MARIA WASHES IN THE DITCH*)
> MARIA LAVA VAVÁ (*MARIA WASHES VAVÁ*)
> VAVÁ FALA (*VAVÁ SPEAKS*)

Until this point, we had got to know five sounds in terms of their graphic representation: TA, LA, FA, MA and VA. The kids had to learn them by heart. They wrote each sound on the tips of each of their fingers – and I'm not ashamed to say that here I resorted to using a short mnemonic: TALAFAMAVA, TALAFAMAVA, TALAFAMAVA, TALAFAMAVA…

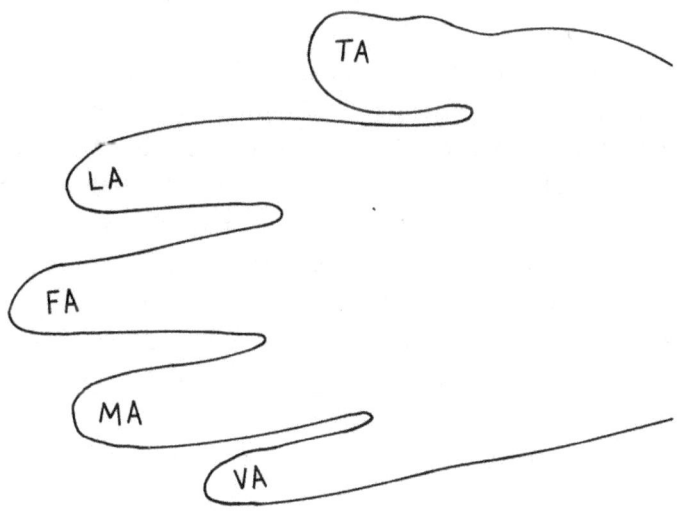

To my mind, the period which began with my very first day in the classroom, until that moment when we achieved the 'VA' sound, stood out as the development of a first stage in my process. I had set out initially with just two lines – one whole, one broken (the hexagram); I had then assigned a non-arbitrary clapping sound to each line; I then substituted these sounds for a phoneme that might be relevant in word-building (TA and LA), and from there I built the word *LATA* (tin can). You might say that until this point all we were doing was playing around with image and sound, and with some mnemonic games alongside them. The introduction of the 'FA' and the word *FALA* (S/he speaks) finally gave me the opportunity to devise some games that were more scenario-based and representational. The 'MA' and 'VA' sounds that followed opened up the possibilities for these kinds of games.

Once I began to see the direction things were going in, and the way the class was responding in a mostly positive manner, I got excited. But perhaps I also started to take things too quickly as a result, because I could sense that I was beginning to divide the class. My relationship with some of the kids was becoming strained: Marilene, Antônio Marcos, Sonia, Rivelino and Adriana, all of whom had been responding well to the process so far, started to get lost, give up or distance themselves. Some regressed to the quasi-mute phase that I'd found them in at the start of the year, whilst others became more aggressive, at times uncontrollable. The initial excitement of my success meant that for almost two months (from May to July), these students were left feeling isolated and forgotten. They couldn't keep up with what we were doing, and I didn't have immediate solutions in the face of their waverings. In August, after the holidays, I decided I would try something new, a more individualized approach.

By contrast, I had been getting particularly enthused by the fact that, after two months of classes, Marcelo, Ronaldo, Sérgio, Alexandre Alves and Jussara were by now all reading everything that I gave them, and fluently. And there was one unforgettable surprise amongst them: Jussara. Jussara had shown signs of autism, and was known for often sitting on the floor at the back of the class and making rowboat movements; I had initially little hope of her coming back from this, given how turned in on herself she was. However, at the first meeting of the Class Council, where I gave an account of my experiences so far, I remember singling Jussara out as someone who had made significant advances. One day, for instance, I had put a phrase up on the board, and all the students had trouble reading it. But surprisingly, Jussara then said:

I'll read it, teacher.

And she read it, with no trouble at all.

I don't recall whether it was in this Class Council or not, but when I told the story to one of the other teachers, he said:

> Leal, write this method down. Your Chinese method is really something.

———

Not everything was coming up roses with class 111. The number of times I complained to myself in my notebook! The entry on 26 April reads:

> I had to miss school today. I feel tired, exhausted, the onset of burnout. I feel completely and utterly consumed by the work, to the point of not being able to breathe or distance myself from it. The demands that Class 111 place on me are absolute, they take up almost all the space in my mind. I worry about the questions of each individual student and how I can help them make progress; I feel the need to study phonetics, phonology, etc.; I feel I must study emancipatory praxis. And whenever I manage to give all these things some semblance of order, whenever I think I have come up with solutions for all the problems I'm dealing with, and I think all is going to be fine – as soon as these things are put to the test of the classroom, within fifteen or twenty minutes of the class I'll have discovered that no theory, no solution, no carefully-planned activity is going to play out as intended. Shit!

But at the end of the day, the decision to work with class 111 was mine. And I had made the decision to work with them from within a state of chaos, not from a state of order – at least the kind of order as prescribed by the *State*. My task was to build order from the chaos.

Perhaps I wasn't yet fully aware of what it meant to work without complete control over one's actions. I was in a hurry, I wanted to see results, the chaos bothered me – and I was beginning to act more like a cop than a teacher, particularly towards José Carlos.

Another diary entry, 18 May 1981:

> Yesterday's drama-based games went terribly. As soon as I'd suggested the first game, all the girls ran off in different directions, and a couple of them left the class altogether. I felt defeated, and continued that way for the rest of the day. Should I maybe avoid working with space and motion on such a big scale with them?

Truthfully, the lack of discipline did get to me. But hadn't I come here precisely to contend with this chaos? I knew there was a contradiction in this. The slightest alteration in my voice, any loss of control on my part, would surprise the kids a lot more than any disagreement among themselves. In that moment they could see that I too was weak, and sometimes they would laugh at me. Kids understand anger all too well. They would allow me to get angry, and even raise the tone of my voice, but they wouldn't allow me to change either myself or my voice – almost like a character in an operetta, in a moment of heightened bad conscience. The act of scolding is necessary, but the nervous alteration of one's tone can actually invalidate the purpose of the scolding, and make it look ridiculous. The rhetoric ends up sounding more like the policeman than the pedagogue.

In any situation where control is lost, I find it best to change track, tune in to other things find new areas of interest – but not to try and hide what it was that caused the loss of control in the first place.

Diary entry, 5 May:

> Despite having made significant progress with the boys, their lack of discipline is severely disrupting the class. José Carlos' provocations are reviving terrible traumas for Alexandre and Clodoaldo.

It seemed to me that my work with both Alexandre Alves and Clodoaldo was having some success, in the sense that our games were beginning to touch upon some of their more fundamental issues.

On 12 May, I wrote:

> Alexandre made some progress today: after we played a kind of truth game, he found himself being listened to respectfully by his peers, having previously been shouted down. He is picking up on these small victories, and is clearly moved and cheered by them.

Two and a half months after the commencement of our classes, Alexandre had won the respect not only of his classmates, but of the whole school.

Clodoaldo would also surprise me at the end of the year, but there was still hard work to be done with José Carlos – I had to intervene in a number of fights between those two. I remember that on one occasion, I had left the classroom to get some cardboard from one of the other teachers' classrooms, and when I returned José Carlos was sitting on the floor, crying, claiming that he had been beaten up by the rest of the class. I immediately asked for an explanation from the others.

> Sure we'll explain, *tio*, but wasn't it you that said that class 111 should be united, like a tribe of Indians, and that if someone attacks one member then the others should return the favour? Well, José Carlos started teasing everyone, then he hit the girls so he got back what he deserved. That's all.

Everyone in the class, girl or boy, had been teased by José Carlos. He was just like that: winding people up the whole time, and even then people tried to pretend that it wasn't going on. He would come over and spit on things, kick stuff around, jab at people with his pencil. And in the end, he always got the reaction he wanted: people hit him back. At least it seemed that was what he wanted. So, what could be done with José Carlos?

———

If by mid-March I had managed to immerse myself in the experiences of Rocinha, without knowing precisely in which direction the work would take me, other than having a few basic ideas in mind, the month of May saw those same paths becoming a lot clearer; certain mistakes were being corrected, and those corrections were being embedded in a network of reference points provided by the practice itself. In turn, what was emerging was a story no longer composed of mosaic, but of much deeper memories, bonds, traces...

It's true that when a relationship is purely professional, not much can be achieved between teacher and student. The proper function of a teacher is to give a class and get the job done. Dictatorships all over the world try to ensure that people take this professional view of the world: the teacher gives classes, the policeman makes arrests, the doctor provides consultations and hands out prescriptions, the soldier engages in warfare, the worker goes to work in the factory. This is how the world turns. The division of labour seems also to divide humanity from the human being: whilst at work, the teacher is a teacher, the policeman is a policeman, the doctor is a doctor. We forget the fact that we are nevertheless human beings all of the time, and that we don't live simply to carry out orders or to fulfil basic functions. And we forget that our humanity is not to be taken for granted, because it is something we fight for on a daily basis, mainly in the way that we produce things and in the things that we produce. In other words, humanity cannot be achieved outside of political practices. At the same time, people cannot conduct their work without affective relations, or without emotion. Without pleasure.

Inevitably, this blend of the practical and the emotional in our human condition can also lead to overlaps between the personal and the professional: most of my students from class 111 knew Manuela, my four-year-old daughter, and Graça, my wife, and now that we were expecting another child, they were always asking if '*tia* Graça's belly was getting really big'. Alexandre Alves had an affection for me that was beyond the norm: he even dreamed that I was his father; Carlos Alberto was one of the first boys to stay at our house, and by the next day he knew my phone number by heart.

At first, I couldn't understand why it was that Carlos Alberto didn't sleep at night, and felt afraid when I turned the lights off. Then he told me:

> It's just that I don't like sleeping at night, *Tio*. Everything is dark. I'm afraid of animals, of ghosts and of bad people.

Then I began to learn why Carlos Alberto was sleeping in my classes. Because at night, he was roaming the bars and restaurants, guarding cars, doing odd-jobs to earn a bit of money:

> If I don't take money home, my mom hits me.

He would spend the whole night out on the street. And he would see in the dawn alone, with eyes wide open.

Carlos Alberto, the young artist, would be one of those who dropped out of class 111. For someone who was up working the whole night, learning was just too tiring. But he never left me. Once in a while, I'd get a fright when the phone rang early in the morning – it was Carlos Alberto, out alone in the world, just wanting to talk, perhaps because I was one of his last points of reference. One night he rang in a state of panic: he'd been arrested by the juvenile court.

> The police have got me, *tio*.

My job always has this visceral dimension, and at times it is like an adventure with no end to it. But I think that it has to be like this. It forces us to find a way to live together, to get angry about things and to fight with emotion and with pain.

TALAFAMAVA had stirred something in the children. I now knew that their learning to read and write could amount to a kind of political and cultural resistance also.

———

All the journeys that I was going on with class 111 necessarily involved my family and friends as well. It was just a given that I would recount what had happened that day or that week, and people were always curious – the conversations I had with Raul, with Helena, with Fernando and Verinha, their suggestions and comments were always valuable.

But Graça was with me the whole time, helping me. When I told her that the kids had come up with the names for two characters, *Vavá* and *Maria Favela*, she helped me to give life to these characters, to create them. That was how we came up with the song 'Fala Maria Favela', which would be revisited regularly over the next few classes:

FALA MARIA FAVELA	SPEAK MARIA FAVELA
TA TA TA	TA TA TA
VIVA MARIA FAVELA	LONG LIVE MARIA FAVELA
LA LA LA	LA LA LA
UM DIA MARIA	ONE DAY MARIA
A LATA VAZIA	THE EMPTY CAN
VAI FALAR	WILL SPEAK

This song brought together the sounds – TALAFAMAVA – with the straight lines, but most importantly it grafted into the kids' imaginations a kind of context in which the action could unfold.

We kept returning to the can-puppet-theatre, where all the puppets would sing behind the curtain. We would continue to work with the combination of sounds that we had learned alongside the new song, bringing them together in the form of words.

The song did present us with various challenges, in the form of sounds that the students hadn't come across before. (To my mind, it is important not to work only with the things that have already been fixed, in the way that they do with students who have been in school for a number of years – as this would be a heresy for special education.) So we had difficulties with the following:

VIVA	LIVE
UM	ONE
DIA	DAY
VAZIA	EMPTY
VAI	GO
FALAR	SPEAK

Evidently, we wouldn't resolve all of these issues at once. But I took the opportunity to begin working on the new vowels, beginning with the E and the I, as in:

FAVELA   VIVA

Then we drew the vowels A, E and I on three fingers of one hand, like so:

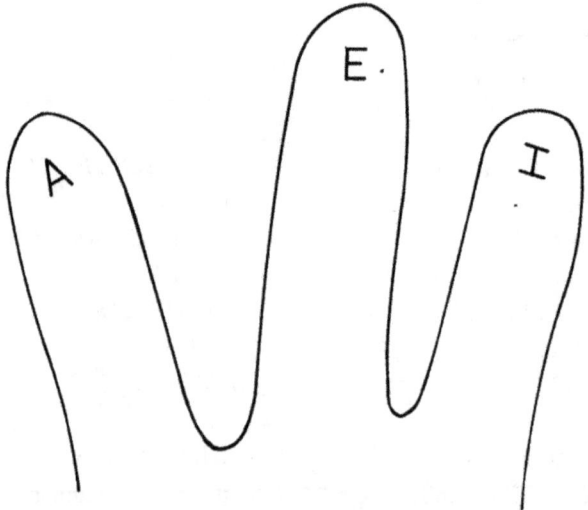

And then words such as:

FAVELA (*FAVELA*)
AME (*S/HE LOVES*)

MATE (*HERBAL TEA*)
LEITE (*MILK*)

And we looked at phrases and expressions such as:

AME A FAVELA (*LOVE THE FAVELA*)
VIVA O VAVÁ (*LONG LIVE VAVÁ*)
A VELA TA NA VALA (*THE CANDLE IS IN THE DITCH*)
A LATA DE LEITE (*THE CAN OF MILK*)

I wanted to work with other letters made up of lines, because I could already envision the need to work eventually not only with all the vowels, but also with consonants that had curved lines. Before working on the curved letters, however, we would have to do some work on simple curved lines. To get to this point, I began by quickly introducing the sound NA into one of the classes:

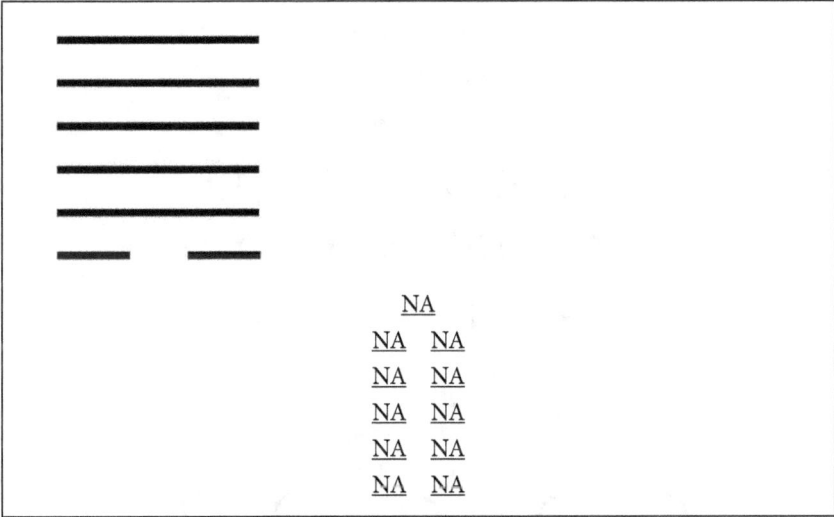

From there, I gave them the name 'ANA':

A	NA
A	NA
A	NA
A	NA
A	NA
A	NA

Finally, I was able to give them the words:

ANA	NU	ANA	NAKED
ANU	NOVE	ANU BIRD	NINE
ALUNO	VENENO	STUDENT	POISON
NAVIO	LONA	SHIP	CANVAS

As well as the games, we also began to do some drawing exercises with curved lines. We played around with circle shapes, mandalas, serpents, etc.

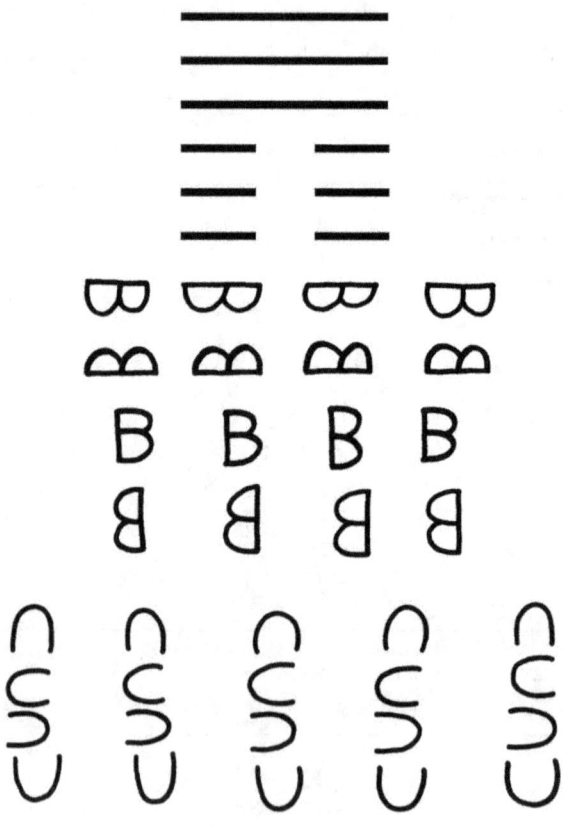

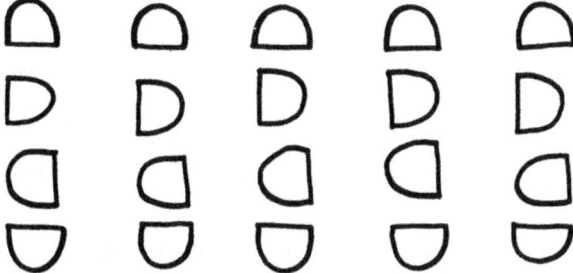

After we'd finished drawing our curved lines, the first sound I gave the kids was 'DA':

DA
DA
DA
DA　DA
DA　DA
DA　DA

And then:

MADAME	DEDO	MADAME	FINGER
DANADO	DADO	ANGRY/DAMN	DICE/GIVEN
DITADO	DONO	SAYING	OWNER
MODA	TUDO	FASHION	EVERYTHING
MOEDA	TODO	COIN	ALL
LODO	LADO	MUD/SLUDGE	SIDE

We then moved on to working with short sections of text, such as the following:

MARIA LAVA NA FAVELA. UM DIA ELA FOI NA MATA. VIU UMA AVE. MATOU ELA E COMEU. E VIU UM OVO E COMEU ELE TODO. DO OVO VEIO VAVÁ, O MENINO DA MARIA FAVELA.	MARIA WASHES IN THE FAVELA. ONE DAY SHE WENT INTO THE WOODS. SHE SAW A BIRD. SHE KILLED AND ATE IT. AND SHE SAW AN EGG AND ATE IT ALL. OUT OF THE EGG CAME VAVÁ, THE SON OF MARIA FAVELA.

MARIA TÁ NA CASA DA MADAME; ELA TÁ COM FOME. MADAME TOU COM FOME. MATA UM HOMEM E COME. MARIA LAVA TUDO, DE NOITE ELA VAI PRA CASA E TEM MEDO DE TUDO. VAVÁ LÊ PRA ELA. MARIA LÊ: TALAFAMAVANADA ELA NÃO TEM MAIS MEDO: TALAFAMAVANADA	MARIA IS AT MADAME'S HOUSE; SHE IS HUNGRY. MADAME I'M HUNGRY. KILL A MAN AND EAT HIM. MARIA WASHES EVERYTHING, AT NIGHT SHE GOES HOME. AND SHE'S AFRAID OF EVERYTHING. VAVÁ READS FOR HER. MARIA READS: TALAFAMAVANADA SHE HAS NO MORE FEAR: TALAFAMAVANADA

I also gave them phrases such as:

1 – VAVÁ É ALUNO DA ESCOLA. 2 – ELE LEVA TUDO PRA CASA. 3 – MARIA FAVELA LÊ COM VAVÁ. 4 – MARIA FAVELA FALA COM VAVÁ E OUVE. 5 – MARIA FAVELA É DOMÉSTICA. 6 – ELE VÊ O NAVIO DA JANELA. 7 – TEM ANU NA FAVELA. 8 – ANA VIU O MENINO NU. 9 – O TETO DA CASA É DE LONA 20 – VIVA O ANO NOVO.	1 – VAVÁ IS A STUDENT FROM THE SCHOOL. 2 – HE TAKES EVERYTHING HOME. 3 – MARIA FAVELA READS WITH VAVÁ. 4 – MARIA FAVELA SPEAKS WITH VAVÁ AND LISTENS. 5 – MARIA FAVELA IS A HOUSEMAID. 6 – HE SEES THE SHIP FROM THE WINDOW. 7 – THERE ARE ANU BIRDS IN THE FAVELA. 8 – ANA SAW THE NAKED BOY. 9 – THE HOUSE'S CEILING IS MADE OF CANVAS 20 – HURRAH FOR THE NEW YEAR.

I even composed a short poem, for them to memorize:

A MENINA DA FAVELA LAVA FALA AMA E LÊ E A MARIA FAVELA VIVE E VAI VIVER	THE GIRL FROM THE FAVELA WASHES SPEAKS LOVES AND READS AND MARIA FAVELA IS ALIVE AND WILL LIVE

NO CORAÇÃO DA MENINA	IN THE HEART OF THE YOUNG GIRL
VAI VIRAR UMA NOVELA	IS A SOAP OPERA WAITING TO HAPPEN
ELA FALA LAVA E AMA	SHE SPEAKS WASHES AND LOVES
COMO A MARIA FAVELA	JUST LIKE MARIA FAVELA
E ELA LÊ O DIA	AND SHE CAN READ THE DAY
FALA ATÉ DA MULATA	AND EVEN TALKS ABOUT THE MULATA[20]
NÃO TEME A VALA E A LAMA	AND FEARS NOT THE DITCH THE MUD
E NEM O TETO DE LATA	OR THE TIN ROOF OVER HER HEAD
É COLEGA DO VAVÁ	SHE IS A FRIEND OF VAVÁ'S
E VAI COM ELE PRA ESCOLA	AND GOES WITH HIM TO SCHOOL
VAI APRENDER CANTAR	SHE WILL LEARN TO SING
COM LÁPIS E PAPEL NA SACOLA	WITH PENCIL AND PAPER IN THE BAG

Towards the end of May or beginning of June, I began to feel the need to stick closer to complete words. When I introduced a new sound, I would always give a series of words that I thought might be important for us. Then, whilst working on the new sounds, I would provide phrases, texts and also poems that I asked them to learn by heart. I thought they would find it more meaningful to encounter poetry in this way – as something alive in their memory. These more complex modes of writing all centred on the story of Maria Favela and Vavá. But that's not what made them so realistic. The tone of the writings was always that of fable, of myth, of the epic – but always referring back to the world of Rocinha.

Despite the school's trumpeting of progressive ideas, its essence always remained the same: the same methods, the same syllabus, the same scaling for assessments, the same murals, the same clichés...

Civics ('Civismo')

Whilst it might seem an inconspicuous and uninfluential sort of a word, the concept of the *civic* actually provides an underpinning to the entire educative

---

[20] A term used to describe someone of mixed race. In this context, the word is more abstract than specific, and likely means that the girl in the poem is the sort of person who will speak up on the part of the marginalized. Historically very common, the usage of the words 'mulatto' and 'mulata' is undergoing some revision in Brazil.

process in Brazil.[21] The school functions within and according to a civic calendar, its murals all portray civic content, and its festivities are civic. In sum, the 'form' of the school is civic.

Put even more simply: the school is a civic space. History is civic, Geography is civic, the social and political organization of the institution is civic, as is its morality – everything is civic. The teachers are civic. The Head is civic. The sporting events are all civic. The school even has a representative student body – The Civic Centre. The school, let's not kid ourselves, is an instrument of propaganda and reproduction of State values. The school belongs neither to the nation nor to the people. It is an instrument of the bureaucratic-civic-military apparatus – one of the modes of oppression that the State exercises over the people.

By contrast: when we speak of educating through *culture*, we mean an education via the things produced by the people. Which is to say, popular education is an education through culture – educating via the customs and practices of the people.

Just as civics calls popular culture[22] into question, so popular culture must call civics into question in return.

Cliché

Cliché-formation is the most fundamental mode of child oppression: its infantilization, its idiotization. The process is quite simple: a preconceived form is given to the sorts of things the child ought to like; from there, a cliché can be formulated, and deployed by adults either as a sort of blueprint for each child (which acts to ensure their future infantilization as adults, their grown-up idiotization), or in the form of games they can mimic, or role-playing and dressing-up. It is up to the child to replicate the blueprint, the image, the copy, the stereotyped design. There is no more effective method for those that want to make of the child not a being, but a future consumer within the wilderness of

---

[21] Leal uses the word 'civismo' as the heading of this section, which literally translates best as 'civility', that is as relating to manners and customs. The adjective used in the rest of the section is 'cívico', which translates as civic, that is as relating to either the city or its citizenry. The use of the word is therefore both politically and morally charged, referring to the kind of citizenship education promoted by the military dictatorship to reinforce the values of the State. Citizenship and civility here are somewhat elided in meaning, with every aspect of the school environment being underpinned by this ideological elision.

[22] Not 'Pop' culture in the Western sense, but the vernacular culture of the people, as contrasted with top-down cultural agendas.

market capitalism. And the school participates in the reproduction of the cliché, embracing the latest thing that the infantilization industry has concocted. In times past this may have been a toybox of flags, of little boats, of prefabricated houses. Nowadays we are more likely to see a coterie of lifeless and largely nameless little animals, or well-known Disney characters. Everything appears transformed into static sticker-album images, pictures with no reality, objects that are purely objectified. And who then really cares about the school supplies and paper industries?

It is by means of this paraphernalia that the child is launched into the world of knowledge: through this particular version of alphabetization the child comes to know itself and the world. This is a world of superheroes, of amorphous and anonymous things, that signify nothing.

Murals

The ideology of oppression is present in the entire visual environment of the school, not least the murals that adorn the refectory, the classrooms and the corridors. These take the form of paintings, of stereotypical Disneyland creatures, of magazine cutouts featuring dinner-table scenes or fashionable people, the beautiful *bourgeoisie* and their world – all of this in captivating kodacolor. This visual language is reproduced in textbooks, in student collages and in their group work. In short, the murals provide a glamorized worldview for all the kids to copy. These kinds of models are disempowering for the young person, both in terms of defining and deciphering their own reality, and in terms of aspiring to the world that the images represent. The world of the school presents itself as a world of murals, of television, of abstract images; the world of the favela is otherwise, and is seen as something to be rejected – something dirty, ugly, discoloured.

We need to work on recognizing the aesthetics of the favela: the bodies of its men and women, their agility, their strength, their sensuality and the expression of their faces and hands. We need to demonstrate the architectural creativity behind the building of the *barracos*,[23] the existence of trees and creatures that fill the gaps between huts and houses, the whole landscape; we need to bring in the image of the *favelados* into the schools. We need to tear down these murals!

---

[23] The simplest form of favela housing construction, usually made from salvaged materials.

A civic episode...

As incredible as it might sound, the police do try to make themselves more popular amongst the people of the favelas. On one occasion, with this idea in mind, the Social and Civic Assistance branch of the Police (ACISO) decided to hold a kind of fête to do with integrating safety into the community. There were clowns, acrobats and other things. There was a show where trained dogs chased bandits, and they had helicopters doing combat demonstrations. The teachers were instructed by the school head, almost compulsorily, to take the kids along to the fair.

I refused to take my students, without offering any further explanation to the head. But the kids soon asked me for one.

> *Tio*, why aren't you taking us to the fête?
> I don't believe in that fête, my boy. Who do you think they will send those police dogs after? Who do you think they will use those helicopters against?
> I've already seen the helicopters attack Denis' family, up there on Road 1.
> That dog has already attacked people from round here. I've seen it...
> I'm not going to the fête, nor am I going to take you. You can do as you please. When class is done, you can go there if you want to...

When the school puts on these civic fêtes, no one asks for the teachers' opinion. I of course have my own: I'm not going to attend any kind of event that I don't believe in.

Sometimes they put on day-long fêtes, sometimes an entire festival week, sometimes an actual campaign event. With the rare exception, these are all embarrassingly terrible.

I remember back in 1980, I took part in 'Oral Hygiene Week', or something along those lines. The school dentist came up to me and said:

> Perhaps, Mr Leal, given your talent for theatre, you could do a little show with the kids.
> I'll do it if I believe in the script.

He gave me the script – needless to say I found it ridiculous. The kids and I came up with an alternative one, one that took their own concrete experience as point of departure. It was met with an aggressive censorship.

> Well, Mr Leal, I think we'd like you to take out this little bit about hunger...

Yes, exactly – you see, Mr Leal, hunger is *not* (as you say) the cause of tooth decay. The cause is a lack of good hygiene. If the kids rinse, they'll have fewer cavities.

The problem – though ideological at its core – was seemingly a lack of information on my part. I got that message loud and clear. I decided it was better to make a few minor alterations and put the show on. Censorship, after all, is best circumvented.

———

Our own theatrical gameplaying was never abandoned, and the randomness of the games actually became the basis for a liberatory pedagogy, in that the game construction didn't proceed according to the will of the teacher, or the wishes of the State, but in tune with the group's collective consciousness, its own expectations. And this consciousness could only emerge out of continuous experience.

Class 111 always wanted to return to particularly memorable exercises. One of them was especially important – albeit somewhat dangerous.

One child would throw himself with arms stretched out onto a tarpaulin held tight by the other kids in the class. Then he'd stay there with his eyes shut. His classmates would fold the tarpaulin over his body and arrange several large sheets of paper around and underneath him (this could be plain or brown paper, or even newspaper). After that, they'd begin unfolding the tarpaulin covering the boy, so that he could then roll himself onto the floor, eventually ending up lying on just the paper, where he'd wait again with eyes closed while someone drew the outline of his body on it with a marker. The boy would then be left to open his eyes and turn to see the imprint left by his body on the paper.

As soon as they began to see its meaning, the kids would play the games amongst themselves, inventing new ideas for the games – gaming the game.

We learn by playing, commented Celso on one occasion.

And they always asked for more games.

———

Ever since my first encounters with the favelas in 1977, I had noticed something deeply significant about the culture there, in that people rarely entertained that ideology around social status and professional mobility that characterizes the middle classes. City-dwelling kids, however poor they are, still always dream of becoming doctors, teachers, soldiers, engineers, etc. I've worked in Madureira, in Osvaldo Cruz – it's always the same. Not so in the favelas. There they live without illusion: kids don't have social aspirations. They want to be stonemasons, carpenters, housemaids, caretakers, etc. You can see this happening at the school: they never play at being teacher and student, doctor, patient, etc.

On the other hand, they are almost always incredibly obedient when it comes to tidying the classroom, clearing up.

The housemaid

The way in which the traditional teacher works with his [sic] favela students reproduces, in a fashion, the way in which he treats his housemaid at home.[24]

In his mind, it is important to cultivate in the housemaid habits and attitudes that pay due respect to their employer's status as boss: punctuality, discrete table service, deference, laundry, cleaning, fulfilment of orders, uniform, living in and keeping one's room tidy, only taking one day off per fortnight, being available for the boss at whatever hour, tidying up, cooking wonderful meals, acting as lady's maid...

Similarly, our students are expected to form habits regarding hygiene, tidying up, cleaning, order, discretion, respect for teachers, etc.

Put another way, the school reproduces in the teacher-student relationship what is essentially a boss-housemaid relation, one founded on servility, slavery, authoritarianism and disrespect for the habits, attitudes and culture of the housemaid.

A teacher with a uniformed housemaid at home is an enemy of the people!

Ultimately, the story of *Maria Favela* is one about lived experiences. She is a housemaid, she has a son who depends on her and doesn't know who his father is. Later on, the kids would discover that Vavá's father works in a factory. At the time he lost his job, Maria wasn't working. She called him a layabout and a

---

[24] Until fairly recently, a large percentage of households in Brazil, from lower-middle income backgrounds upwards, employed domestic staff (with many continuing to do so). Housemaids would live in their patron's house or apartment (in the 'quarto de empregada') and serve them anytime. They often wouldn't share toilets with the patrons, and, in most of the Copacabana buildings, for example, they had their own lift/elevator and should use the 'service door'. Leal's critique in this section is of bourgeois morality (particularly among fellow teachers), not of those who seek this employ.

number of other things, because he wasn't bringing any food home. He left and never came back.

This story rings true because it reflects the stories of so many of my students, whose mothers are housemaids and whose fathers work in factories.

To awaken the consciousnesses of these kids to the world of work, and maybe even to de-condition them from servile labour, we would have to devise a lot more games, activities and scenarios. We would have to build houses out of newspaper, string, chairs and tables. We would make machines using our own bodies, with each person comprising a component of that machine. We'd devise our own fêtes, build our own favelas. After all, how would Rocinha herself have been built?

We began with some improvisation work, reproducing the teacher-student relationship in the classroom, rotating the roles, and following the activities up with discussion of the tasks, in which I also took part.

We also improvised some other scenarios around the oppressor-oppressed relation, rotating the roles once again.

These activities provided us with the opportunity to discuss some important questions, like the division of labour, the ability of all to make a contribution, the boss-employee relationship, the order-giver vs. the order-taker, the different kinds of work done by the kids' parents (from working on the land to working in the city).

We also talked about the lack of jobs, going on strike, and the favela vagrants, who were usually casual labourers or entirely unemployed.

Only creative work can be truly liberatory, as it contributes to the creation of the individual:

> What sorts of things could we create from our tin cans?, I'd ask the children.

All of the experiences gained via these classroom activities were discussed and channelled via the developing story of Maria Favela.

Every time I presented the children with a new sound, I would give them a series of around ten words and about five or six phrases to go with them.

These sentences had seemed to me to be absolutely essential, ever since our very first word: 'the tin can talks'. It is by means of the sentence that the whole narrative, dramatic and historical nexus is developed – the whole life of the class. It is not the only factor, of course, because we also have the other units: the drawing of the letters, the words, the story. Each class entailed various exercises – completion, creation, dictation – that had as their touchstone a letter chart, a sound chart or even just a chart of crossing lines, in which the children had to find words. For example:

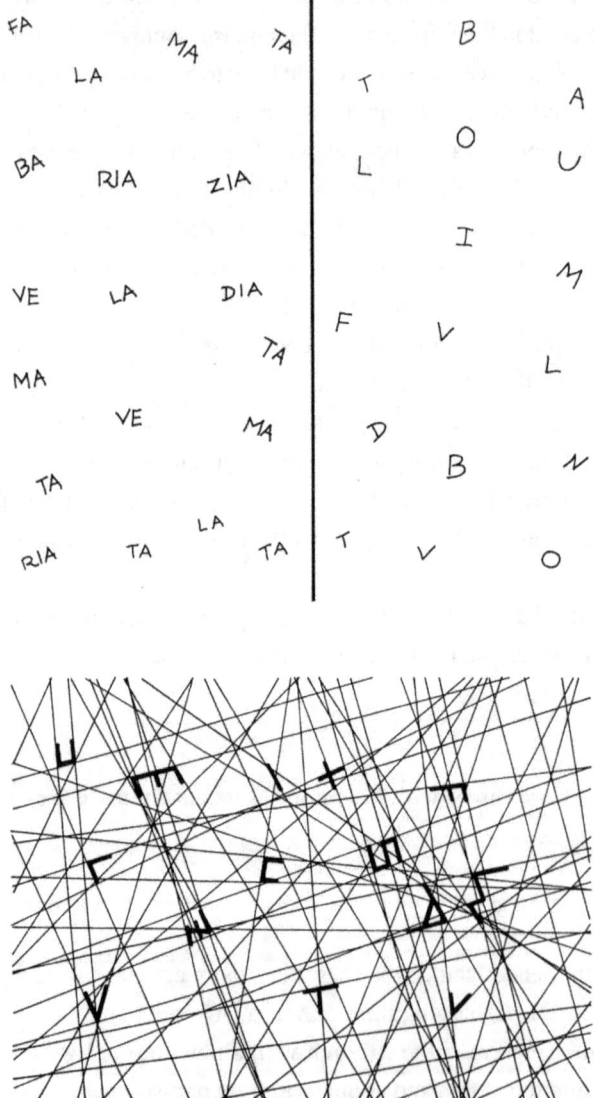

The drawing games and exercises, as with the role-playing games, are as infinite as our willingness to explore them. It is the same with the written word: even if the printing press succeeded in creating a stereotype of the graphic world, there are innumerable resources at our disposal for rediscovering the threads of writing's fabric.

I introduced the students to the sounds PA and BA in just the same way as I had with the other letters:

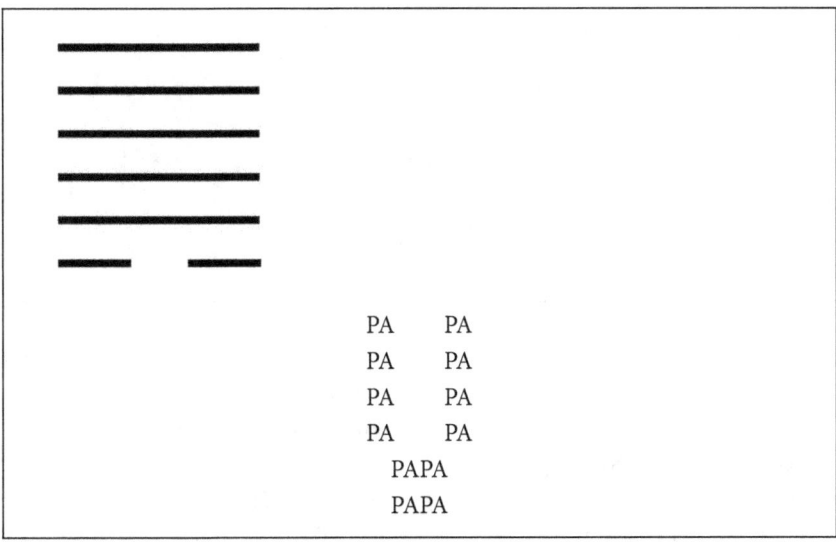

PAPA	PIPA		POPE	KITE
PAI	PICO		FATHER	PEAK
PELADA	PEDIDO		SOCCER GAME	REQUEST
PATO	PETECA		DUCK	SHUTTLECOCK
PULO	PODE		JUMP	IS ABLE
PEITO	PITADA		CHEST	PINCH
POLÍCIA			POLICE	

They would then read:

1 – MARIA VIU O PAPA.	1 – MARIA SAW THE POPE.
2 – O POVO PODE TUDO.	2 – THE PEOPLE CAN DO EVERYTHING.
3 – A PIPA VOOU.	3 – THE KITE FLEW.
4 – ELE PULOU A VALA.	4 – HE JUMPED THE DITCH.
5 – O PAI DELE É DA POLÍCIA.	5 – HIS FATHER IS IN THE POLICE.

```
             ▬▬▬   ▬▬▬
             ▬▬▬   ▬▬▬
             ▬▬▬▬▬▬▬▬▬
             ▬▬▬▬▬▬▬▬▬
             ▬▬▬▬▬▬▬▬▬

                          BA
                          BA
                          BA
                   BA     LA
                   BA     LA
                   BA     LA
```

BALA	BOLA	BULLET	BALL
BOTECO	BETO	BAR	BETO (Name)
BODE	BANANA	GOAT	BANANA
BOA	TABA	GOOD	TRIBE
TÁBUA	BONITO	BOARD	BEAUTIFUL
BAILA	BOTA	DANCE	BOOT

Then read:

A MENINA FOI NO BAILE.	THE GIRL WENT TO THE BALL.
A BANANA TÁ BOA.	THE BANANA IS GOOD.
A FAVELA É MUITO BONITA.	THE FAVELA IS VERY BEAUTIFUL.
A TÁBUA BATEU NO PÉ DO MENINO.	THE BOARD HIT THE BOY'S FOOT.
O TIME DO BOTAFOGO É BOM DE BOLA.	BOTAFOGO IS A GOOD FOOTBALL TEAM.

The texts always had a story-like tone to them. This narrative style mixes myth and reality, and the moral message is almost always in evidence: the important thing is to show the favela as a place of fortitude and not of fear, to generate love for the place and its people – for the ghetto...

That was how this small piece composed around the PA and BA sounds came about.

They would read:

O PAPA TEVE NA FAVELA. MARIA VÊ A NOVELA E VÊ A BALA MATANDO ELE. ELA VIU O PAPA. VIU A PISTOLA E TEVE MEDO	*THE POPE WAS IN THE FAVELA. MARIA WATCHES THE SOAP OPERA AND SEES THE BULLET KILLING HIM. SHE SAW THE POPE. SHE SAW THE PISTOL AND WAS AFRAID.*
TALAFAMAVANADA PA BA TALAFAMAVANADA PA BA TALAFAMAVANADA PA BA	*TALAFAMAVANADA PA BA* *TALAFAMAVANADA PA BA* *TALAFAMAVANADA PA BA*

By this time, we were about to enter the month of July, and the holidays were approaching. The kids and I began some work on geometric shapes, drawing on my reading of a work by Paul Klee. Straight lines, curved lines and now shapes – we were still in the realm of the graphic, even if it had been infiltrated by geometry. With the June festivals still going on, I decided to work with the kids on some June-related themes. We decorated the classroom, came up with ideas for the school fête, designed rockets and fireworks, balloons and lanterns, flags, campfires and other things.

I preferred to use just a simple pencil for the outlines of these designs, and then we filled in the gaps of each of the objects with paper cut from stencils and then glued on. We made a hot air balloon to release on the June festival day, but, for various reasons, it never got finished. It was a white balloon on which each of the children had put their initials, filling in the gaps in the letters in coloured cutouts of their choice. The sounds we'd been working on – PA and BA – were particularly in tune with the June festivities, the sounds of fireworks and rockets. The grand opening of a popular festival, which usually blends elements of sound, sculpture and theatre, also opens the imagination to all sorts of new avenues. At the same time, the game-playing that takes place, invented by the people, has its own set of rules according to which each person is then able to improvise. A popular festival contains all the world's games, even the unconscious ones – it is the human-as-a-whole at play.

That fete was really important to class 111. It was held outside the school grounds, closer to the favela, and the kids entered into their gameplaying in totally untethered fashion, coming and going randomly, bumping into others here and there. The kids from my class got together with those from other classes to dance a *quadrilha*.[25] And because only 111 had rehearsed the *quadrilha*, they took the initiative and encouraged others to join.

Now that the festival was done, the term was about to end. I wrote some sentences up on the board that the kids had provided for me, despite their containing some sounds that were still unknown to them:

1 – TEVE FESTA NA ESCOLA.	*1 – THERE WAS A PARTY AT THE SCHOOL.*
2 – TEVE BARRACA, BOMBA E CAIPIRA.	*2 – THERE WERE STALLS, FIRECRACKERS AND KIDS IN FANCY DRESS.*[26]
3 – A 111 FEZ UM BALÃO.	*3 – CLASS 111 MADE A BALLOON.*
4 – O BALÃO É BRANCO.	*4 – THE BALLOON IS WHITE.*
5 – A 111 DANÇOU NA FESTA.	*5 – CLASS 111 DANCED AT THE PARTY.*
6 – TODOS OS MENINOS COLARAM BANDEIRINHAS.	*6 – ALL THE KIDS GLUED LITTLE FLAGS TOGETHER.*
7 – VAVÁ FOI NA FESTA COM MARIA.	*7 – VAVÁ WAS AT THE PARTY WITH MARIA.*
8 – TEVE LEILÃO.	*8 – THERE WAS AN AUCTION.*
9 – MARIA LEVOU BOLO DE AIPIM.	*9 – MARIA BROUGHT CASSAVA CAKE.*
10 – BETO TIROU UMA BOLA NA PESCARIA.	*10 – BETO FISHED A BALL FROM THE FISHING GAME.*

Overall, the first semester had been a deep dive.

On 12 March, I had commented in my notebook: 'I know nothing. I just have a handful of clear ideas that I can start with', ideas that were outlined by the end

---

[25] A dance adapted from the much earlier European *quadrille*, or 'square dance', and which emulates traditional wedding dances.
[26] The word 'Caipira' translates more accurately as 'Yokel', 'Bumpkin' or 'Hillbilly', referring to the countrywide tradition of dressing up as farmers for the festivals of St John the Baptist. Despite pejorative connotations in English, children across Brazil still dress as these characters for the festival of São João, although there are increasingly moves away from the affectation of country life.

of that month in a vague concept of *alphabetization*. By this last day of semester, the experience had thrown open a thousand new horizons, reference points, joys and stories.

Now, at this final stage of the school year, I was less concerned with enjoying and recounting these successes, and more with my mistakes.

I was aware that my work with the group had, on the whole, been good. The kids were beginning to form strong bonds with one another, they respected one another more, and they understood the value of what was happening in class 111.

The question for me now was how to reintegrate the broken links in our chain. I'll explain: the progress of class 111 had been at the expense of some kids who hadn't been able to keep up. As a result, they tended to act up, turning their back on the class, and sometimes staying away from school altogether. Some were beginning to miss more classes than usual.

What was needed now was a deeper engagement with individual issues through personalized work for more than half the class, whilst also diversifying the group work for the half that was most behind. I would have to divide them into two groups. Furthermore, there were students, such as Alexandre Alves, who had come a long way in the literacy process, but whose behaviour required individual attention. By behaviour I mean less a mode of discipline, than a way of life. Alexandre was already a well-behaved boy from a disciplinary perspective. But what he needed now was to take stock of the steps he had taken to get where he was, in producing letters and discovering words. That kid needed retrieving from a lack of self-awareness, pulling back from the abyss.

To make a success of this more individualized approach in the second semester, I would have to invest more fully in each student's backstory, and come up with games that would enable them to increasingly develop their selves, and not just their skills. What's more, I decided to ask for assistance, whether from the Helena Antipoff 'technical' team, or the Department of Education and Culture, or anywhere willing to provide it, via the school's guidance counsellor. There was at least one student that I didn't think myself up to the task of teaching: José Carlos.

What I needed right now was not someone to sort all of my students' problems for me, but someone with the right psychological training who would be genuinely interested in researching alongside me the various ways of working with this or that child. And from there, it would maybe give me the opportunity to work on my own.

But all the efforts made by the school guidance counsellor were in vain. The school's institutional approach to psychological matters only operated at the level of bureaucracy, and almost entirely on the side of bureaucracy, providing it with its alienating, dominant discourse.

So, with half the school year gone, I was dwelling on my many mistakes, flaws and failings. I had thought, for example, that it might be possible to *alphabetize* the students' parents via their children's books. What a utopian dream! Only in the story of Maria Favela can Vavá alphabetize his own mother. And shouldn't that be sufficient?

We had also tried to make a balloon, which we ended up not finishing. I had picked up on the problems Antônio Marcos was having, but I didn't act quickly enough.

And on the question of spelling, I hadn't even figured out my own position. I disagreed with the spelling guidance provided for us by the Helena Antipoff Institute, so I followed it out of a sense of tact rather than of conscience: at times I would provide the accents for words, when I thought that they would not generate confusion, but at others I left the accents off. I'd put punctuation in, and then leave it out, and sometimes I'd make deliberate spelling mistakes: writing '*ome*' and not '*homem*' (man). In the beginning, the matter of size and positioning of letters hadn't bothered me. But come July, the kids had started to use their lined notebooks, and I chose not to interfere in the 'correction' of their letters.

At the same time, I was beginning to think about the matter of the capital letters that I had been teaching the kids to draw. If I was getting them to write each letter as an individual entity in a word, wasn't I contributing to the idea of the ABC as script of the masses instead of the expression of the unique child, which is more pronounced in their own cursive handwriting?

I also made an intuitive decision not to ignore curse-words – because why shouldn't the kids write 'jerk' or 'bust-up' if it was appropriate? To my mind, using curse-words in the classroom was a mode of people's true expression.

In the end, I questioned whether all the mistakes, flaws and failings that had been made need be thought of as a matter of self-blame? Instead, I decided to treat them as material that could be reworked, and not as abominations to be consigned to oblivion.

Right now, I felt the need to deepen the work I had been doing on the inclusion of class 111's cultural background: I needed to seek out the songs from their communities and sing with the kids, to develop stories with the kids themselves, talking about Rocinha, their lives, bringing in new characters (bad guys as well as good), constructed from the familiar faces of their own community. These new characters would become Maria Favela's antagonists within our theatrical gameplaying. Out of all this would emerge a new primer, containing all this material plus the stuff that was in the kids' textbooks, a primer that would be produced by the hands of children, and not by a typewriter or photocopier. I felt as if the kids were tired of copying exercises out of a book; at the same time, there was not enough well-organized material from which they could learn independently. This primer seemed to me like the only way to go.

I'd also take the kids to the school library, however dangerous an idea that might be. They needed to know how to handle books. That said, the last books to be handled by children should be textbooks – textbooks are the kind of tonic for children that leaves them with a bad taste for reading.

One final thing that I thought important to work into the second semester's activities was more a kind of general knowledge: knowledge of the body, of the origins of the favelas, of the division of labour, of migration, etc. The kids are always curious to learn new things, and they need to know that the world is not structured in as immutable a fashion as those in power present it to be.

The children returned to their first class in August with zeal, the class buzzing with chatter and stories. I told them about the birth of my son, Pedro Germano, and they wanted to know how it had gone. After the experience with Pedro, I knew a lot about how babies were born, as I had been helping Graça during a drawn-out labour, so I was keen to tell the kids everything. I remember that Alexandre Alves took this opportunity to recount the grimmest aspects of childbirth imaginable.

In this first class, we went back to telling stories, as we had been doing at times during the first semester. I told a story – or rather, I read out a story that I'd written back in May, called 'Queen of Beauty, Giant of the Wind'. But most of the class was distracted by other things, and not paying attention to my story. In fact, I don't think they much cared for the stories I told them. So I decided to ask whether any of them would like to tell a story instead. Ana Paula was the first to come forward, and the class was enthralled. She told stories that she'd made up herself, entirely from her own imagination. There were common themes running through the stories: they always featured pregnant women, the characters were exclusively female and the narrative always involved the appearance of an animal – a stray dog, or a pig – that by means of a spell would interfere with the birth of the child, causing it to be born with the face of a dog or a pig, and thus contaminating the whole family.

These were surrealist tales, and they enchanted the children. The silence produced by Ana Paula's stories was total. These were children that loved to tell stories about werewolves and other horrors that they'd seen on television, late at night. And they were afraid.

Up until the middle of August I continued to work with the whole class. We moved onto the sound 'RA/RRA': the 'RA' mimicking the sound of an animal's roar, and the 'RRA' emulating the engine of a car. I stuck two large boards up on the wall of the classroom: one with a tiger on it, another with a car. Then I turned on the tape recorder, with noises made by a car and a tiger on it, and presented to them the 'RA' and 'RRA' sounds:

RA	RRA	RA PA	FA RRA
RA	RRA	RA PA	FA RRA
RA	RRA	RA PA	FA RRA
RA	RRA	RA PA	FA RRA
RA	RRA	RA PA	FA RRA
RAPA FARRA		COP[27] PARTY	
RIVELINO TERRA		*RIVELINO LAND*	
RODA CARRO		*WHEEL CAR*	
RÁDIO PORRADA		*RADIO BEATING*	
RETA FERRO		*STRAIGHT LINE IRON*	

So that they could then read:

1 – O RIVELINO RI À TOA.	1 – *RIVELINO LAUGHS POINTLESSLY.*
2 – TEM RATO NO BARRACO.	2 – *THERE IS A RAT IN THE SHED.*
3 – NÓS VIVEMOS NA TERRA.	3 – *WE LIVE ON EARTH.*
4 – NÓS VIVEMOS DA TERRA.	4 – *WE LIVE OFF THE LAND.*
5 – ELE IRRITA A RITA.	5 – *HE IRRITATES RITA.*
6 – O OME DEU PORRADA NO MENINO.	6 – *THE MAN GAVE THE BOY A BEATING.*

[27] More specifically, a policeperson that seizes goods from unlicensed street vendors. The word has a number of other meanings in Brazilian and Portuguese, but this is the most likely given the family of words around it.

In the second half of August, I decided to put into practice both some of the individualized work, and work with the class divided into different groups. Two students would come to school each day, a half hour before class began, to do some individualized work with me. At the same time, I divided the class into two groups, one of which wouldn't come to school on the Tuesdays, and the other not coming on the Wednesday. This seemed to be the best solution, because it is impossible to have four or five activities going on in the same classroom when you want to make progress with everyone. With that kind of multi-tasking, the kids that are most far behind often just get given simple games or other distractions that mean very little to them, and in classes that have a lot of problems, a wide range of activities create almost insuperable class management issues. Initially the school board suggested that all the kids still come to class, but that a colleague join me to work with one group whilst I was with the other. For whatever reason, this didn't happen, and the fact that the board ended up 'allowing' the kids to not come to school one day a week is just further proof that school boards needn't behave monolithically, and can be persuaded – if not trampled into submission – by the new, the transformational.

―――

I never got to know Antônio Marcos's back-story all that well. He was the son of a former school caretaker, and he had a sister who was also illiterate. His behaviour could swing from an effusive affection when doing something which made him happy, to an out-of-control, borderline convulsiveness, when he was provoked, or couldn't understand something, like the reading or writing.

In the first two or three months of the school year, Antônio was a happy boy. But when we moved to written work, he got lost.

I told a friend about Antônio:

He writes back-to-front...

I was told that Antônio was dyslexic. Parentheses: we have a tendency to label people according to their illnesses, and illness – as bad as it may be – is always significantly lesser than the person themselves. In science, the human being has been treated effectively as the disease, as its object. Medical professionals, then, reproduce this same ideology: they treat people as diseases to be cured...

Here is the outline of the class I prepared for Antônio Marcos on 21 August:

• grande/pequeno	• *big/small*
• esquerdo/direito	• *left/right*
• frente/atrás	• *front/back*
• LA – esquerda	• *LA – left*
• TA – direita	• *TA – right*
• TA – direita	• *TA – right*
• LA – esquerda	• *LA – left*

CÓPIA *COPY*

Illness/hunger/madness

If it is not possible to say substantively that humans are a disease in themselves, they are everywhere described as such in adjectival form, by hunger and by collective madness in their endemic state. These are evils that beset and afflict the people of the *favela*.

In the favela we find the safe-and-sound, the save-those-who-can-save-themselves…

… and the thousands of drowned?

There are the apathetic, the aphasic, the drunk, the tubercular, the malnourished, the silly, the crazy, the meek, the dumb, the monosyllabic, the marginalized, the semi-clothed, the phantasmagorical, the deformed, the paralyzed, the underfed, the enslaved, those that feed on leftovers, those that feed off pig swill, the lame, the defective, the toothless, the irrational, the contagious, the fearful, the ones with the bulging eyes, the pickpockets, the muggers, the rascals, the pestilent, the exhausted, the brute-forceful, the illogical, the slowly dying, the dwarves, the monsters, the blind, the ideologically blind, the infamous, the perverts, the asexual, the violated women, the women for whom rape is the only form of sex, the sterile, the saintly and the demonic, the city-wanderers, the parentless, the curtain-twitchers, the surfers with afro hair full of paraffin, the people who want to be other people, the people that dirty the plate they are eating from, the night-wanderers, those who are not living but hiding, those who are effectively dead because they never make an appearance, the illiterate, those that never speak in black-and-white, the asses, the donkeys,

Illness/Hunger/Madness

the people who pick through trash, the barrowmen and their amazing cargo, the childish, the every-other-day-DIYers, the scouts, the smokers, the see-no-evils, the ditch-divers, the trash-dogs, the identity-cardless men and women, the identity-less, the idle, the isolated, the beastly, the burrowing...

———

The individualized tasks were carried out either in the form of exercises proposed by me, or in conversation with each child.

What follows is an example of a class copied verbatim from my notebook, and intended for that half of the class that wasn't progressing with their reading and writing.

I – Breathing exercise:
   a) Students should breathe in and out whilst repeating the word 'cachorrinho' (puppy), reading the hexagram to produce the rhythm of their breaths, a number of times:

They do this on their own at first, then as a group.
   b) Students should breathe calmly, filling their lungs with air and releasing it slowly. Thoracic breathing.

II – Play and games:
   a) LET'S SEE WHO WINS THE BLOWING CONTEST.
   b) EXHALING WHILE SAYING THE VOWELS.
   c) RELEASING THE AIR AGGRESSIVELY.
   d) SHOUTING.
   e) CALLING THE PERSON AT THE CENTRE OF THE GROUP NAMES: WITH EVERY NAME-CALLING, HE WILL RESPOND WITH TA LA FA MA VA NA DA

III – Relaxing.
IV – Experimenting with touch, with space, with eyes closed.
V – Evaluation.

Classes with this group were always playful. Nevertheless, at the end of the first semester they were complaining. They wanted more games. They liked to learn through play and were very much aware of the fact.

The school was plagued by a particular image of itself, and this wasn't just one beset with issues of madness, hunger and disease – an image of chronic problems. No, the problem was bigger, extending to the way in which the State continued to reinforce the way of life in the favela, by means of an apparatus that was more than just the military police. What we are talking about is the institution of violence as a way of life.

Violence

In the name of crimefighting, they [i.e. the State] come into the favelas, persecuting and killing people, disrespecting civil and human rights, creating a climate of war and fear, whilst no one has any right to appeal. The techniques deployed range from those acquired by the military apparatus through their experience in subversive combat, spying, information technology, the 'blitz', annihilation (torture, killing, etc.), to much older strategies that had served the European colonizers in their own modes of extermination: playing families and tribes off against each other, generating hostilities between the oppressed of one favela and those of another.

And this had also been the recent history of Rocinha. One police chief (who, incidentally, would be promoted again and again for services provided within his 'Public Security Secretariat'), in addition to using sophisticated methods against local 'bandits', joined with one of these rebel groups, covered for them and then launched them against the Road 1 Group, considered the good rebels, the true heroes of the people of Rocinha. These police-rebel actions and alliances are known throughout the favela, including by my students.

I remember that this police chief, in a full-page interview in the *O Globo* newspaper, spoke about popular resistance to the rebels within the favela, when in fact it was he who had orchestrated the face-off between them.

This kind of institutionalized State violence ensures that any authentic popular resistance within the favelas is impossible: no one shelters the rebels, no one respects the pact of not robbing those within the favelas, the myth of the rebel as a hero of the weak is destroyed and the residents of any one street are afraid to cross over into the neighbouring one. Hate is cultivated between people, through fear and through denunciation – a true state of terror.

It's important to talk about violence, in every classroom: representing and analysing what is going on. I had already started to work on these subjects in the texts dictated by the children. Ana Paula read out the following:

O DOCA É LEGAL. ELE DÁ DINHEIRO E PAGA DOCE PARA AS CRIANÇAS. PAPAI GOSTA DO DOCA. O PESSOAL TODO GOSTA DELE. ELE É UM HOMEM RESPEITADO: NÃO FALA PALAVRÃO. NÃO FUMA MACONHA PERTO DAS CRIANÇAS E RESPEITA TUDO MUNDO. ELE PARECE OF CHEFE DO PEDAÇO. O DOCA TEM UMA FILHINHA.	*DOCA IS COOL. HE GIVES PEOPLE MONEY AND PAYS FOR SWEETS FOR THE KIDS. DADDY LIKES DOCA. EVERYONE LIKES HIM. HE IS A RESPECTED MAN: HE DOESN'T SWEAR, DOESN'T SMOKE POT NEAR THE KIDS AND RESPECTS EVERYONE. HE LOOKS LIKE THE BOSS OF THE PLACE. DOCA HAS A YOUNG DAUGHTER.*

This text, which contains some difficult words, would be presented at the end of the year. Ana Paula decided to take the text to Doca himself, as a kind of gift from someone who had learned to read and write. She reported that he had read the text slowly.

> Tell your teacher not to meddle in my life: he could be a police informant, using the kids to get dirt on us…

That was Doca's message to me. Some of the students' mothers felt the same: they told me not to make the kids write things down in their notebooks.

———

The findings I'd make from September onwards wouldn't be particularly huge, at least at the level of writing. In this I was perhaps, once again, making a mistake: with the class split into two groups, one more advanced than the other, I was seeking to work quicker on the literacy skills of those who easily absorbed the new sounds. This may explain why I neither invested as much time in graphic research nor made progress with researching sound. And it would also prevent against the unification of the whole class any time soon.

The three days per week that the kids all came together were given over to playing, to singing, to acting and to building the primer. With this entire group, I would work on games, music, theatre and books. With the group that was more behind, I would devise specific games and go over the basics of sound and graphics. With the more advanced group, I would continue with the alphabetization process, providing them with new sounds, devising texts, reading, interpreting and doing dictation.

On being provided with the sounds 'SA', 'CA', 'GA' and 'JA', they were given a new text:

MARIA VEIO DA BAHIA. ELA CASOU, O HOMEM DELA PERDEU O EMPREGO E FOI EMBORA DE CASA.
VAVÁ DISSE:
   QUEM É MEU PAI?
E ELA RESPONDEU:
   VOCÊ NASCEU DO OVO.
	MARIA CAME FROM BAHIA. SHE MARRIED, HER HUSBAND LOST HIS JOB AND LEFT HOME.
	VAVÁ SAID:
	   WHO IS MY FATHER?
	AND SHE ANSWERED:
	   YOU WERE BORN FROM AN EGG.

ELE NÃO É BOBO E DISSE PRA MARIA:
   MENTIRA...
   TEU PAI É OPERÁRIO. O SALÁRIO NÃO DAVA PRA SE VIVER. ELE SE FOI...
   MAMÃE, ONDE FICA A BAHIA?
	HE IS NOT A FOOL AND SAID TO MARIA:
	   THAT'S A LIE...
	   YOUR FATHER IS A FACTORY WORKER, THE SALARY WASN'T ENOUGH TO GET BY. HE LEFT...
	   MOMMY, WHERE IS BAHIA?

VAVÁ FICA PERGUNTANDO TUDO. MARIA FAVELA LAVA A ROUPA.	VAVÁ KEEPS QUESTIONING EVERYTHING. MARIA FAVELA WASHES CLOTHES.

Where is Bahia? I decided to pose this question as a way into addressing the issue of immigration in class. I then showed the kids a map of Brazil and pointed to the state of Bahia. I had to explain what a map was – an outline of a very large place, reduced to a certain size. Rocinha couldn't even be seen on the map, being so small in comparison to either Brazil or the State of Bahia. Why then did people from other States, who lived on farms, in much bigger places, come to Rocinha? I touched on the issue of land ownership, and the low salaries paid in those areas – I explained that, at times, jobs are entirely unsalaried.

Almost all the people that came from Bahia, Pernambuco or other States used to work on the land. When they get here, what do they do? Work on construction sites, in rich people's houses, as handymen... and a large number simply never find work. And those who have no job, we call them bums or thieves, don't we?

That same day, I managed to get a map of Brazil for each child. I told them to find out from their father or mother the State they had come from, and mark it with a pencil on the map. In the next class, when they brought back their answers, we began to compare Rocinha with their parents' place of origin. We arrived at various conclusions: in Rocinha, at least their homes were their own, and they had a school nearby; on the other hand, it was still necessary to dig pipeline trenches to guarantee water for all, and find jobs for everyone.

We began to develop some short texts about Rocinha. Here are some of them:

O BOIADEIRO	BOIADEIRO
O LARGO DO BOIADEIRO É O PRINCIPAL LUGAR DA ROCINHA. VENDE DE TUDO: FRUTAS, FEJÃO, CARNE. QUEM COMPRA SÃO OS PRÓPRIOS MORADORES NORDESTINOS E MINEIROS. DOMINGO TEM FEIRA. MUITA GENTE VAI NA FEIRA DEPOIS DA MISSA.	BOIADEIRO IS THE MAIN SQUARE IN ROCINHA. IT SELLS EVERYTHING: FRUITS, BEANS, MEAT. THE BUYERS ARE THE PEOPLE FROM THE NORTH-EAST AND MINAS. ON SUNDAY THERE'S A MARKET, A LOT OF PEOPLE GO TO THE MARKET AFTER MASS.
O RUIM É QUE NÃO TEM NENHUM FESTA NO BOIADEIRO.	THE BAD THING IS THAT THERE ARE NO PARTIES IN THE SQUARE.

A PEDRA DA GÁVEA A PEDRA DA GÁVEA É A COISA MAIS LINDA DA ROCINHA. QUANDO ELA TEM ALGUMA NUVEM PRETA EM CIMA DELA É MAU SINAL. DIZEM QUE VAI ACONTECER COISA RUIM. SERÁ QUE A PEDRA DA GÁVEA PROTÉGÉ O PESSOAL DA ROCINHA CONTRA A INJUSTIÇA E QUE UNE TODO MUNDO QUE NEM A 111?	THE ROCK OF GÁVEA[28] THE ROCK OF GÁVEA IS THE MOST BEAUTIFUL THING IN ROCINHA. WHEN THERE ARE BLACK CLOUDS ON IT, IT IS A BAD SIGN. THEY SAY THAT BAD THINGS WILL HAPPEN. DOES GÁVEA'S ROCK PROTECT ROCINHA'S PEOPLE AGAINST INJUSTICE AND UNITE EVERYONE, IN THE SAME WAY THAT CLASS 111 IS UNITED?
NO TERREIRO TEM TERREIRO, MAIS DE CEM, NA ROCINHA. A NOSSA CASA, O NOSSO BARRACO, FICA PERTO DE UM. MINHA MÃE RECEBE ESPÍRITO. ELA GOSTA DO PAI-DE-SANTO DO CENTRO. TODO MUNDO CONVERSA SOBRE A VIDA E DIZEM: SARAVÁ, MEU PAI.	IN THE TERREIRO[29] THERE ARE MORE THAN ONE HUNDRED TERREIROS IN ROCINHA. OUR HOUSE, OUR HUT, IS NEAR ONE. MY MOTHER RECEIVES THE SPIRIT. SHE LIKES THE PAI-DE-SANTO OF THE CENTER. ALL THE PEOPLE TALK ABOUT THEIR LIFE AND SAY: SARAVÁ,[30] MY FATHER.

Politics

Just changing our minds does little to change our selves: the immutable order of the world will always be upheld if we don't change our behaviours.

A lot of historical facts can pass us by without leaving much of an impression: few people will remember Getúlio Vargas,[31] the coup of 1964, the guerrilla uprising of 1968, the dark days of the decade of dictatorship in the 1970s, the São Paulo ABC strikes of 1978, or even more recent events concerning ourselves, such as the teachers' strikes of 1979 and 1980, that spread to the whole of Brazil...

---

[28] A monolithic mountain in Tijuca Forest, above Rio de Janeiro. The rock formation at the top of the mountain is said to resemble a human face.
[29] A place of worship for Afro-Brazilian religions.
[30] A greeting in the Afro-Brazilian religious tradition.
[31] Brazilian politician, social reformer and president of the country from 1930 to 1945, and again from 1951 to 1954.

(The habits and attitudes of a certain kind of stereotypical teacher from the 1960s could easily gloss over these historical facts. But historical processes are more complicated than their – often superstructural – facts. If these changes didn't leave their mark on many, others were felt by all: the hippy movement, sexual liberation, the revolutionary typology, consumerism, etc.)

What, though, was the effect of the teachers' strikes, at the level of structural change in schools?

'The CEP[32] is us!' With this slogan, we became the teachers' movement that drove the school strikes. And the strike is in turn the biggest of all schools, because it unbalances our habits and attitudes and causes rapid changes in behaviour.

There are two CEPs today: there is the one that I recognize, a grassroots teachers' movement; then there is the other CEP, comprised of a bureaucratic and power-hungry leadership, grasping for positions in legislative assemblies.

Politics can be the preserve of spokespersons, or of political professionals. Our voices have to be put into action on a daily basis, which is to say that politics is the most important instrument of our working lives; it is inalienable, and transformative of our behaviours.

We are the CEP, and the CEP is us; we are the school, and the school is us; we are the teachers' movement, and that movement is the transformation of the school itself.

The political superstructure – governments, political parties, etc. – these are not what change History. The world is transformed when we strike at the heart of what seems *beyond* change: the prevailing modes of production and the governing orders of behaviour.

Transforming the school today means a transformation of the ideological discourse of the dominant classes (in which the teacher is presently clothed), into a new cultural expression of resistance by the oppressed classes, a language that the teacher will have to learn.

———

But let's return to Paula Brito School specifically. If it were the case that all teachers, advisers and supervisors reflected on their training, and on their own function within the school's division of labour, and if they had a good grasp of the activities of the CEP through years 1978 to the present day, including

---

[32] Centro Estadual de Profissionais de Ensino do Rio de Janeiro (State Center for Teaching Professionals of Rio de Janeiro).

the teachers' strikes, and most importantly if they had a good understanding of their own performance in the classroom and how to transform it, alongside the transformation of the lives and struggles of the *favelados* – then meaningful change to their practice would certainly take place.

Nevertheless, it seems to me that Paula Brito did begin a shift in the second semester of 1981, primarily in the way it was structuring its strategic plan for 1982. This shift began with a large number of meetings, in which teachers, advisors and supervisors, as well as external stakeholders, all participated. From the meetings, we moved almost unconsciously into working on school practices, focusing on community data distributed via handout, and on the personal experiences of some of the teachers, particularly those undergoing their professional development in the 1981 school year.

Although the language and tone of the strategic plan is still 'pedagoguese', within it already lie the marked intersections with transformative practice. And even though the plan doesn't state exactly how it means to go about achieving its goals, one of the main objectives of the plan is for everyone to participate in the school's decision-making processes.

Another objective is the use of both general and specific methodologies, derived from a critical reflection upon practices experienced in the UE.[33] To achieve this aim, the plan proposes to bring together first-grade teachers and community-based educators, as well as conducting both individual and collective evaluations.

The plan aims to stimulate research into, and use of, methodologies that are fit for popular education practices grounded in community culture research and studies into each year group and subject. The intention is also to establish systematic contact with parents and with other institutions that serve the community. And finally, the plan aims to give priority care to the first grade.

With the signatures of a large number of teachers attached, the plan is not to be underestimated. Nor can we underestimate the requirement for teachers to participate in the kinds of meetings being held. My own participation in the development of the strategic plan was also important, and I say this neither with false modesty nor without recognition of the contributions from various other teachers, but rather as proof that a teacher's practice is never limited to the classroom; if the teacher's practice is fully transformative, the winds of transformation will blow through the entire school, however hard the fight to make that happen might be.

---

[33] Unidade de Ensino – the 'unit of teaching' refers to the planned approaches to teaching and learning activities for any given stage of school (kindergarten, elementary, etc.).

This account also demonstrates that the teacher's political role must be constantly evolving, in motion and ready to move others in the struggle for a better school, for better working conditions and for better pay. What's more, this is a struggle that cannot be left to an institution simply working on behalf of teachers – it must be led by the teachers themselves.

———

In the classroom of 111, Ana Paula took control of storytelling, Paulo José – whose body was near electric – dominated the dancing and the fighting, and Carlos Alberto commanded the drawing. But the person who best understood music was Márcio.

Ever since my time doing theatre work in schools back in 1977, I had been researching the songs sung in Rocinha, songs that never made it to the radio, but with which I sometimes surprised the students by singing. These ranged from Cirandas to unedited Sambas, but also included well-known songs with the lyrics changed and spiced up.

I had previously always drawn on these songs for my theatre work, but now with class 111 they would actually be sung – in particular to make the most of Márcio's enthusiasm. Four songs would be included in the kids' final primer, so it is important to make a note of them here.

The first two songs *Maria Linda Maria* and *Vida de Pobre* were originally performed by students for a school concert in 1977, at Paula Brito. These are the songs:

MARIA LINDA MARIA	MARIA, BEAUTIFUL MARIA
Ô, Ô, MARIA, Ô, Ô, MARIA (BIS)	OH MARIA, OH, OH MARIA
MARIA MENINA ALEGRIA	MARIA, GIRL OF GREAT JOY
MARIA TRABALHADEIRA	HARD-WORKING MARIA
MARIA LINDA MARIA	MARIA, BEAUTIFUL MARIA
MARIA MAIS COMPANHEIRA	MARIA, LIFE'S GREAT COMPANION
MARIA VIVE FELIZ	MARIA WHO LIVES HAPPILY
MARIA VIDA CERTEIRA	MARIA OF THE STABLE PATH
MARIA MORA NO MATO	MARIA, LADY OF THE FOREST
DO LADO DA CACHOEIRA	AT THE SIDE OF THE WATERFALL
MARIA QUE SABE AMAR	MARIA WHO KNOWS HOW TO LOVE
MARIA MENINA FACEIRA	MARIA, THAT CHEERY GIRL
MARIA NEM SE QUIMAR	WHO CAN JUMP THROUGH FIRE
MARIA PULA FOGUEIRA	WITHOUT GETTING BURNED
MARIA ME LEVA CONTIGO	MARIA TAKE ME WITH YOU

VAMOS DESCER A LADEIRA MARIA CONTIGO EU CONSIGO TAPAR O SOL COM A PENEIRA MARIA DOS OLHOS CASTANHOS MARIA FLOR DA ROSEIRA MARIA TE CONHECI DEBAIXO DO PÊ DA FIGUEIRA MARIA DORME FELIZ DEITADA NUMA ESTEIRA	WE'LL GET DOWN THE HILL MARIA, WITH YOU I CAN MAKE THE WORLD SEEM BRIGHTER MARIA, MY BROWN-EYED GIRL MY ROSE PLUCKED FROM THE TREE MARIA, I FIRST KNEW YOU UNDER THE FOOT OF THE FIG TREE AND NOW YOU SLEEP HAPPILY STRETCHED OUT ON THE STRAW MAT

VIDA DE POBRE Ó QUE VIDA AMARGURADA O POBRE TRABALHA O ANO INTEIRO TRABALHA, TRABALHA, E NÃO TEM NADA NO FIM DO MÊS TEM QUE PAGAR A PRESTAÇÃO DO PADEIRO, DO AÇOUGUEIRO E OUTRA VEZ FICA DEVENDO FICA DEVENDO AO PATRÃO MAS QUANDO CHEGA O CARNAVAL QUER FANTASIA PARA BRINCAR LAIÁ LAIÁ SÃO TRÊS DIAS DE FOLIA E VOLTAR PRA TRABALHAR MAIS UM ANO SEM PARAR	THE POOR MAN'S LIFE O, WHAT A BITTER LIFE THE POOR MAN WORKS THE YEAR ROUND, WORKS AND WORKS, BUT HAS NOTHING AT THE END OF THE MONTH HE HAS INSTALMENTS TO PAY TO THE BAKER, TO THE BUTCHER BUT YET AGAIN HE IS IN DEBT IN DEBT TO HIS BOSS BUT WHEN CARNIVAL ARRIVES FANTASY COMES OUT TO PLAY LAIÁ LAIÁ IT'S THREE DAYS OF MERRYMAKING AND THEN BACK TO WORK ANOTHER YEAR WITHOUT A BREAK

Of the other two songs – the first was also created for a school concert, and the other came from an anonymous composer. Here they are:

NA ROCINHA SÓ EXISTE UM PORÉM NÃO SE PODE CONVERSAR	IN ROCINHA WE EXIST AS ONE PERSON AND YET NO ONE CAN HAVE A CHAT

PERTO DE NINGUÉM FICAM DE LONGE A ESPIAR CORRE LÁ NO POSTO VAI CAGUETAR CORUJÃO MORREU DE PESCOÇO TORTO DE TANTO CORUJAR A VIDA DOS OUTROS LUCI, LUCINHA MINHA NÓS VAMOS CASAR E SAIR DESSA ROCINHA (BIS) SENTADO NA CADEIRA CONTAREI PARA VOCÊ NÃO ME DEIXE TÃO SOZINHO PORQUE SENÃO EU VOU MORRER	NEAR TO ANYONE ELSE THERE ARE THOSE WHO ARE STANDING BY TO SPY, TO REPORT BACK TO THE STATION TO INFORM ON EVERYONE ELSE OL' OWL HAS DIED OF A CROOKED NECK FROM SO MUCH OGLING AT THE LIVES OF OTHERS MY LUCI, MY LUCINHA WE'LL GET MARRIED AND GET OUT OF THIS PLACE (BIS) SITTING ON THIS CHAIR I WILL TELL YOU NOT TO LEAVE ME SO ALONE BECAUSE OTHERWISE I WILL DIE
TRABALHO MUITO MAS SEM FALTA DE CONFORTO MORO NO MORRO SEM NECESSIDADE SOU POBRE NÃO POSSO MORAR NA CIDADE DELEGADO ME PRENDEU COMISSÁRIO ME SOLTOU DEIXA DE PRENDER MALANDRO PRA PRENDER TRABALHADOR ME CHAMARAM LADRÃO SOU LADRÃO PORQUE EU POSSO METO A MÃO NUMA PEIXEIRA MINHA VIDA É PRA NEGÓCIO AI BOTINA SAPATO SEM MEIA NÃO COMBINA	I WORK HARD BUT I DO NOT WANT FOR COMFORT I LIVE IN THE FAVELA WITHOUT GREAT NEED I AM POOR, I CANNOT LIVE IN THE CITY THE POLICE OFFICER ARRESTED ME THE POLICE COMMISSIONER RELEASED ME STOP HOLDING THE RASCAL TO ARREST THE WORKER THEY CALLED ME THIEF I AM A THIEF BECAUSE I CAN BE I KEEP ONE HAND ON MY FILLETING KNIFE MY LIFE IS OPEN FOR BUSINESS OH, THESE BOOTS THESE SHOES WITHOUT SOCKS DO NOT WORK

I carried out individualized work with nine of the kids, over two months. My intention here was to make them aware of their own particular shortcomings, and to help them discover avenues for overcoming them. I had no intention of becoming a psychologist. All I knew of psychology was as much as a theatre teacher should know – after all, each of us has something in them of the poet, the doctor, the psychologist, the madman, etc.

I already mentioned the work I had tried to do with Antônio Marcos. I had a few books on mirroring exercises, so we did some of those; the others I just invented. In truth, I didn't much care for the books' exercises, which always seemed to propose orthopaedic solutions, when the problems weren't actually physical, nor were they a matter of the person's birth, or a consequence of neurological damage. They arose from matters of family and of society. As such, they could be worked on more effectively via discussion and gameplaying.

Towards the end of September/beginning of October, Carlos Alberto was no longer coming to school. He and Alexandre Alves had taught me a lot. These were two super-problematic children, but also super-aware. Both of them would say:

I'm the one with the best head on my shoulders in the family.

They would even try and solve their own family issues. Carlos Alberto lived constantly in search of a wandering brother who, according to him, was thieving wherever he went.

> If the police get him, teacher, they'll kill him. I have to find him and stop him from stealing.
> My mum is worse. You know her, sir. As soon as I arrive home, she's hitting me for everything I do and for doing nothing. And she even makes me eat rotten food.

Carlos Alberto's mum was an alcoholic. He had no dad. He was the one that had to earn the family income, either keeping an eye on people's cars for them or unloading groceries for supermarkets at night.

Within the family, there would never be a place for Carlos Alberto. Outside of it, he was destined either for the FUNABEM,[34] or mendicancy, or ...

---

[34] Fundação Nacional do Bem-Estar do Menor (National Foundation for the Well-being of Minors). Despite the name, the institution evoked here was akin to a Juvenile Detention Centre.

In his family, Alexandre Alves almost certainly had the best head on his shoulders. He had already experienced a number of tragedies: he saw his uncle kill his father, who was a criminal; he may also have been present at the death of his two brothers (under what circumstances I don't know). And it seemed that whenever something tragic happened in Rocinha, Alexandre Alves was there – he witnessed, for instance, a mother killing her own child, right after it had been born.

I managed to have a word with his mother on one occasion. She was as lucid as her son, but equally as immersed in so many tragic events that she wept any time they came up. She felt let down by the school.

> Last year they sent me a note saying that I had to take the boy to the doctor because he was crazy. My son isn't crazy. The school disgusts me.

Alexandre's mum even talked about ending her own life. She told me that she drinks, which allowed her to get along with the other people living around her. She is friends with a lot of criminals. Her candid and lucid demeanour had made her a kind of messianic leader.

Alexandre loves his mum, but he is aware of her limitations. She is unable to maintain a home for her children, and she drinks too much.

When I asked Alexandre to invite his guardian to the school, he didn't go to his mother, but to his auntie Maria, who took care of him. I talked to her a lot. Alexandre was very content living with her. I remember that when I went to go and photograph him with his family, we took the picture outside auntie Maria's house, along with her kids.

Maria complained about some of Alexandre's bad habits, but she also adopted a very maternal and protective attitude towards him. He clearly loved her, and vice versa. I spoke plenty with Alexandre in those two months. He said that he would prefer to live with his auntie Maria than his crazy grandfather.

All the work we had been doing over the school year had resulted in some visible improvements in Alexandre's behaviour. In October, he was borderline literate, if only he hadn't then come down with mumps for a twenty-day period. Alexandre was ultimately a very sweet boy, very attentive, and now also a lot less aggressive.

———

I never set out to write a dramatic piece with the children that had *Maria Favela* as its protagonist. Even now, in terms of her story, we only had a few basic facts about Maria, and these had been provided to make her feel like a real person. Now I decided it was time to begin creating an antagonist for Maria Favela, with the children's help – a character that would confront her. I was becoming increasingly fascinated with puppets at this time, and was even in the process of writing my own puppet 'epic'. This was why we'd made our tin can puppets – even if they were pretty flimsy (if we'd tried to build anything more elaborate, we'd have run out of time for anything else, as class time is so short).

It was actually Alexandre Alves who rummaged around in the collective unconscious, and in his own, to reveal a version of the *Blonde Lady*[35] – only this time she was based on the real story of a woman who three or four years previously had appeared in a public school, seemingly with the intention of attacking the kids. A lot of schools will already have forgotten about the [original story of the] *Blonde Lady*. But the fact of this more recent event having really happened seemed to guarantee its survival, its canonization – or better, its *mythification* within favela schools such as Paula Brito.

> But who is this *Blonde Lady*?, I asked the class, wanting to probe for characteristics of *Maria Favela*'s antagonist. Only Alexandre gave me more than ten characteristics, but all the other kids were animated by talk of the *Blonde Lady*. So I set about noting down their observations, almost as an automatic writing exercise:
> - she wears a red outfit down to her feet;
> - she lives at sea;
> - she wears pyjamas;
> - she used to live inside the flower;
> - she was red but turned white because she fell into a bag of flour;
> - she is only scary during the daytime;
> - she lives in a house full of flowers and cobwebs;
> - she takes from the rich to give to the poor;
> - come and find out who killed her;
> - Gilberto, who lives near me, says that we have to say to her: take the cotton from your daughter! Then she leaves;

---

[35] An urban legend of a female spirit who appears upon invocation with blonde hair, white clothes and pieces of cotton in her ears, mouth and nostrils. The myth is said to have originated in the nineteenth-century story of Maria Augusta de Oliveira, who fled from a forced marriage to Europe, where she was said to have died of rabies, aged twenty-six. Also referred to as the 'Bathroom Lady', or 'Cotton Lady', she was known to appear to children in school and public bathrooms, due to a school having been built on top of her tomb.

- her brother-in-law killed her;
- she died of seventeen stab wounds;
- she took four cactuses, buttered them and ate them;
- she made cotton and cotton-candy;
- she was a DEC teacher;
- she was a teacher, she earned money; she did not like money, she cooked it in the pot and ate it;
- when she laughed her vampire teeth would appear;
- you didn't die because you are back here again;
- she lived in a coffin;
- she carried a pocket knife in her pocket;
- the pocket knife fell down the drain;
- she killed animals: spiders, mice, cockroaches;
- lightning on her belt buckle was what killed the animals;
- she died in the bathroom;
- she took off her clothes;
- bugs wanted to catch her;
- she had no eyes, only holes;
- she was a sea witch;
- she said: hi Dona Lígia, you are beautiful;
- she opens the door with her mouth or with the pocket knife;
- she became a cook, and made poisoned food;
- the bathroom ceiling is covered in cotton wool.

So now Maria Favela had a fully formed enemy. We fashioned various *Blonde Ladies* out of tin cans. We did some improvisation work, letting the situations happen freely. At the end of the classes, we would always talk things through, trying to build on the information we had gathered. But I had no intention of creating a finished script. Perhaps I'll come back to that one day.

I recall one particular improvisation sequence we did, which had as a theme: 'Up above sits Rocinha, below the Hotel Nacional'. At the very end, I presented them with the sound 'XA', one of the last basic sounds to learn. The presentation of the sound was slightly unusual. I wrote out the poem 'LUXO LIXO'[36] on a black belt with silver lettering, like so:

---

[36] A visual poem by Augusto de Campos, a key figure in Brazil's concrete poetry movement of the 1950s, in which the words 'LUXO' (Luxury) and 'LIXO' (Trash) are mutually signifying.

```
LUXO      LUXO  LUXO            LUXO    LUXO  LUXO LUXO
LUXO         LUXO   LUXO            LUXO    LUXO  LUXO LUXO
LUXO         LUXO    LUXO    LUXO    LUXO              LUXO
LUXO         LUXO        LUXO                LUXO         LUXO
LUXO         LUXO        LUXO  LUXO         LUXO         LUXO
LUXO  LUXO   LUXO     LUXO       LUXO       LUXO         LUXO
LUXO LUXO  LUXO  LUXO         LUXO       LUXO LUXO LUXO
```

XA
———
XE
———
XI
———
XO
———
XU
———

Leia:

XEPA
DEIXA
PUXA
LUXO

From the poem we got the sounds:

XA
XE
XI
XO
XU

Then they had to read:

XEPA (*LEFTOVERS*)
DEIXA (*LEAVE*)
PUXA (*PULL*)
LUXO (*LUXURY*)

The school had a number of typewriters, which could be used for any course being given at the time. It was on these machines that the children and I typed out the first pages of our very own primer. This posed no difficulty for them: the keys were all exactly like the letters they had been working with.

The texts were taken directly from their notebooks. I tried to get them to do some drawings on carbon paper that could be included in the primer, but this would take too much time, when we were already in the second half of October. We did some drawings that ended up not being used, and took advantage instead of some that had already been produced on a typewriter. Finally, we put them through the manual printing machine together.

The majority of the textbook's sixty-two pages had been put together by myself and my wife, Graça. On the day that I gave each child their copy of the primer, a book that they themselves had put together, we threw a real party. I had brought a box of coloured pencils for each of them, so that they could colour their book as they liked.

I was only able to make three trips to the library with Class 111. I remember the way Ana Paula said:

Tio, the books are so beautiful! They're giving me goosebumps.

It was true – she was really overcome. For Ana Paula, a book was a sacred object, a treasured object.

To my mind, pre-fabricated primers and textbooks are the greatest enemies of a real book.

I also believe that, prior to their experience of textbooks, kids need to handle art books, books with just pictures in them, books that foster their creativity, story books. These are books appreciated as treasured objects, but put to use in the same way as a toy.

Textbooks are truly boring objects that always give the same lessons. They stipulate what has to be done, the duties of the reader, the kind of copying to be carried out. They are all an abomination.

'XA' would be the penultimate basic sound I'd give to class 111, the final one being 'ZA'. To facilitate the fixing of the sounds already learned, we continued the onomatopoeic formula:

TA LA FA MA VA NA DA PA BA RA SA CA GA JA XA ZA

With the group that was more behind, I set as limit-objective a basic knowledge of these sounds with variant vowels. If they could read and write words built out of these basic sounds, they would already be practising a form of literacy.

With the more advanced group, I also worked on the sounds CHA LHA NHA AN AM AR AL and TRA FRA DRA PRA BRA CRA GRA. Here is some of the graphic work we did with these final sounds:

TRAbalho FRAça GRAna

PalaVRA

CRUz GRAnde TRAça

BRAsil

LOOKING FOR WORKERS WITH PRACTICAL EXPERIENCE.
LOOKING FOR WORKERS WITH PRACTICAL EXPERIENCE.
LOOKING FOR WORKERS WITH PRACTICAL EXPERIENCE.
LOOKING FOR WORKERS WITH PRACTICAL EXPERIENCE.
LOOKING FOR WORKERS WITH PRACTICAL EXPERIENCE.
LOOKING FOR WORKERS WITH PRACTICAL EXPERIENCE.
LOOKING FOR WORKERS WITH PRACTICAL EXPERIENCE.
LOOKING FOR WORKERS WITH PRACTICAL EXPERIENCE.
LOOKING FOR WORKERS WITH PRACTICAL EXPERIENCE.
LOOKING FOR WORKERS WITH PRACTICAL EXPERIENCE.

The graphic exercises at the end of the year were drawn from newspaper headlines, which I asked the kids to copy out. We then set to work dramatizing the headlines. I also asked them to copy out pieces of graffiti, either simple words or graphic symbols. It's usually the case that these words are written out in stick-like capital letters, with variant strokes. A lot of the kids were 'self-teaching' this kind of font for themselves at the same time...!

I have already said something about how our stories had a moral to them. In the favelas, there is a lack of literature that really conveys the lives of the people there, that draws from the imaginary of this people's collective unconscious. I wrote a tale for the children that also appears in their primer. It was one of our last readings as a class:

FÁBULA	A TALE
TINHA UM POÇO NA FAVELA, DAVA PRA VER A ROCINHA REFLETIDA NA ÁGUA. TODO MUNDO VINHA VER A SUA CARA DANÇANDO NA ÁGUA DAQUELE POÇO.	THERE WAS A WELL IN THE FAVELA, IN WHICH YOU COULD SEE ROCINHA REFLECTED IN THE WATER. EVERYONE CAME TO SEE THEIR FACE DANCING IN THE WATER.

UM DIA VEIO UM HOMEM DE LONGE E CUSPIU DENTRO E TODO MUNDO COMEÇOU A CUSPIR DENTRO DO POÇO E A FAZER OUTRAS PORCARIAS QUE FORAM SUJANDO O ESPELHO DA ÁGUA! NINGUÉM MAIS VIA A ROCINHA NEM A SI MESMO NO FUNDO POÇO. E COMEÇOU A FALTAR ÁGUA PRA BEBER.
O HOMEM QUE VEIO DE LONGE DISSE:
    A ROCINHA NÃO PRESTA.
 	
E TODO MUNDO QUE MORAVA NA ROCINHA REPETIU:
    A ROCINHA NÃO PRESTA, SENHOR FORASTEIRO.
	ONE DAY A MAN CAME FROM FAR AWAY AND SPAT INSIDE AND EVERYBODY STARTED TO SPIT INSIDE THE WELL AND TO MAKE OTHER KINDS OF MESS THAT DIRTIED THE MIRROR OF WATER! NO ONE COULD SEE ROCINHA OR THEMSELVES IN THE WELL ANY MORE. AND THERE WAS A SHORTAGE OF WATER TO DRINK.
	THE MAN WHO CAME FROM AFAR SAID:
	    ROCINHA SUCKS.
	
	AND EVERYBODY THAT LIVED IN ROCINHA REPEATED:
	    ROCINHA SUCKS, MISTER OUTSIDER.

Our class was on occasion invaded by students from other classes, who were curious to see what was going on, especially when the kids were improvising with the puppet theatre. Mírian, a former student of mine who was now in the 5th grade, started dropping into class 111, drawn either by the theatre or by her desire to flirt with one of the boys in the class – Alexandre Gomes, a blond eleven-year-old who sang like a rooster. Her attendance, at first sporadic, soon became routine, even when her love for Alexandre faded. She was actually enough at ease to help her peers with their reading.

This was such a beautiful example of solidarity. Beyond offering her own assistance, she was able to show the students how to help one another. And so it was: the more advanced kids in the class began to spontaneously help out those that were more behind. The acts of learning and teaching were becoming ownerless, teacherless and a lot of progress was being made as a result. The enthusiasm generated in this final spurt would see Celso, Jurandir and Marcio all achieved basic reading and writing skills. One day Celso called me over to read a phrase that he had written out himself:

ATOPAFALACUMEUPAICIVAVAMIJANACAMA

It came out exactly like that, all stuck together, but meaning: Will you speak to my dad about *Vavá* pissing in the bed?

The school year was far too short to bring to fruition all that was going on between October and September. It was only at the very end of the year that Clodoaldo, Alexandre Calixto and Paulo José started to read their first words, but there was now little time for this newfound passion to grow. I was sitting at a desk in the middle of the classroom when Clodoaldo started to read an unknown phrase from the board. I got so excited that I suddenly said to the others, crying:

Look everyone, Clodoaldo is reading.
Ha, *tio* is crying – said one of the kids. Total silence fell on the classroom, and then all the children started clapping.

———

Whichever way you look at it, the achievements of my work were no miracle, and could only be described as modest. Of the twenty-six students that began class 111, nine either attended infrequently or not at all, three made almost no progress, three were on the verge of basic literacy but fell short because things clicked into place just before the end of term, and eleven of them achieved basic reading and writing skills.

There were three days remaining before classes ended, and I called Fábio from the Residents' Association to talk to the class about the Association and what it meant for Rocinha.

On that day, I also presented the final text to go into the kids' primers, the last chapter of the story of *Maria Favela* for that year.

MARIA FAVELA FALA MARIA NÃO DIZIA NADA. VAVÁ ENSINOU ELA A LER E A FICAR PERGUNTANDO TUDO. AGORA MARIA ESTÁ MAIS FORTE. HOJE É DOMINGO DE MANHÃ, ELA ESTÁ NA ASSOCIAÇÃO DE MORADORES DA ROCINHA. MARIA FAVELA FALA. VAVÁ FICA BRINCANDO DE VIVO-MORTO.	A VOICE FOR MARIA FAVELA MARIA USED TO NOT SAY ANYTHING. VAVÁ TAUGHT HER TO READ AND TO KEEP QUESTIONING EVERYTHING. NOW MARIA IS STRONGER. TODAY IS SUNDAY MORNING, SHE IS AT THE RESIDENTS' ASSOCIATION OF ROCINHA. MARIA FAVELA HAS A VOICE. VAVÁ IS PLAYING AT VIVO-MORTO.

Index

Abertura Política 43, 43 n.16
abstract/abstraction 2–3, 7, 24, 30, 37, 57 n.20, 59
ACISO (Social and Civic Assistance branch of the Police) 60
Advisory Committee on Special Education 25, 27–8
aesthetics 59
Afro-Brazilian 80 nn.29–30
alfabetização (becoming literate) 2, 7
alfabetizar (teaching literacy) 2–3
'Alive-Dead, Dead-Alive' game 10 n.7, 23
alphabet 2–4, 7, 12, 29
  alphabetize/alphabetization 2, 34, 41, 59, 69–70, 78
  true alphabet 7
architectural creativity 59
attendance at Special Education classes 28
authentic/authenticity 77
authoritarian/authoritarianism 9, 22, 28, 41, 62

Barata, F. 7
barracos 59
Blonde Lady 88–9
Boal, A. 10
  200 Exercícios e Jogos para o Ator e o Não Ator com Vontade de Dizer Algo Através do Teatro 10 n.8
boss-employee/housemaid relationship 62–3
bourgeoisie 59
  bourgeois morality 62 n.24
Brazil 8, 43 n.16, 57 n.20, 58, 62 n.24, 68 n.26, 79–80
  Afro-Brazilian 80 nn.29–30
  Brazilian-Portuguese 40 n.15, 72 n.27
  households in 62 n.24
  Rocinha (*see* Rocinha, Rio de Janeiro (Brazil))
  Tijuca Forest mountain 80 n.28

bureaucracy 2, 26–7, 41, 70, 81
  bureaucratic-civic-military apparatus 58

Caipira festival 68 n.26
Campos, A. de 89 n.36
Campos, H. de 7, 7 n.4
censorship 60–1
CEP 81
citizenship 58 n.21
civic (civismo) 57–8, 58 n.21, 60–2
  civic fêtes 60
The Civic Centre 58
civility 58 n.21
clapping system 21–2, 31, 35, 46, 94
Class Council project 44, 46–7
community 22, 22 n.10, 25, 43–57, 60, 70, 82
  community work 43
  primitive 44
  school-community relationship 43
conscious/consciousness 3, 10, 12–13, 43, 61, 63. *See also* unconscious minds
constructivism 8
creation 2–3, 16, 25, 38, 63–4
creative/creativity 2–3, 12, 16, 27, 32–3, 59, 63, 91
  architectural 59
  creative literacy 19
  creative practices 42
culture 29, 33, 43–4, 58, 58 n.22, 61–2, 82
curriculum 42

decision-making processes 22, 82
de Silveira, N., *The Museum of the Unconscious* 8
dictatorship 43 n.16, 49, 58 n.21, 80
disease 25, 73–4, 76
domestic chores of children 19, 36
dominant class 32, 44, 81
drama-based games 33, 47
drawing game 9, 16, 18, 20, 34, 54–5, 64, 90

education/educational discourse 13, 18, 22, 25, 27–9, 58
　citizenship 58, 58 n.21
　educational reforms 43 n.16
　impaired 26–7
　popular 58, 82
　reading and writing 1, 7, 14–15, 21, 24, 28, 34, 46, 67, 71, 73, 75, 78, 92–4
　Special Education (*see* Special Education/Special Educational Needs)
emotions 17, 49–50
environment 1, 58 n.21, 59
Escola Paula Brito school 1, 22, 24, 27, 43, 81–3, 88
　Artistic Education initiative 22
　Schools Support project 22, 43
　Special Education class 1, 26
'Escola Sustentação' (School Support) project 43
esoteric/esoterism 16
evaluation 26, 76, 82
exercises 7, 9, 11, 14, 19, 23–4, 27, 29, 33–4, 54, 58, 61, 64, 71, 75, 86, 88
　automatic writing 88–9
　breathing 75
　graffiti 92
　graphic 92
experiences 2–4, 7, 13, 22–3, 26–7, 41–3, 46, 49, 60–3, 69, 71, 76, 82, 87, 91

family 9, 13–14, 17–25, 50, 60, 71, 72 n.27, 86–7
Farofa (traditional Brazilian side dish) 39 n.14
favela. *See* Rocinha, Rio de Janeiro (Brazil)
favelados 13, 59, 82
Freinet, C. 4
Freire, P. 4, 10 n.8, 13, 37
　Education as the Practice of Freedom 4
　generative words 13, 13 n.9
　The Pedagogy of the Oppressed 4, 13 n.9
Fundação Nacional do Bem-Estar do Menor (National Foundation for the Well-being of Minors) 86 n.34

games 1–2, 8–12, 21–2, 24, 29, 41–3, 48, 54, 58, 61, 63, 67, 69, 73, 75–6, 78. *See also* play/playing
　'Alive-Dead, Dead-Alive' 10 n.7, 23
　can-puppet 38, 51

drama-based 33, 47
drawing 9, 16, 18, 20, 34, 54–5, 64, 90
gameplaying 10–11, 31, 61, 67–8, 71, 86
　game-within-the-game 11
　graphic 15, 19, 21, 78
　mnemonic 46
　'Pass the Ring' 29, 29 n.12
　primordial 10
　role-playing 58, 64
　school fête (June festivals) 67
　spontaneous 11
　theatrical 11, 61, 70–1
　'Vivo-Morto, Morto-Vivo' 23
general knowledge 71
generative words 13, 13 n.9

hands, human 21, 24, 29–30
hexagrams 14–17, 19–21, 31, 35, 38, 46, 75
housemaids 62–74
housing construction of favela 59 n.23
human being 49, 73
　humanity 13, 49
hunger 25, 60–1, 74–6

I Ching (Chinese book of divination) 14–16, 34
ideogram 2, 7
illness 73–6
imagination 3, 33, 51, 67, 71
infantilization 58–9
inhabitants 44

Klee, P. 14, 67

labour 13–14, 19, 29, 33, 49, 63, 71, 81
languages 1, 3, 13, 17, 27, 37, 41, 59, 81–2
　phrases 37–40, 45–6, 53, 56–7, 63, 93–4
　visual 59
　vocabulary 28
　vowels 52–3, 75, 91
liberatory practices (political practices) 42, 61
literacy 1, 9, 13, 18–19, 22, 37, 69, 78, 91, 94
　teachers/teaching 2–4, 7, 10, 12, 17, 19, 22, 26–7, 41
　word-based 12, 26–7
literature 1, 17, 42, 92
lumpenproletariat 27

madness 74–6
marginality/marginalization 22, 25–6, 29, 34, 40, 57 n.20, 74
Maria Favela (character) 41, 45, 51, 57, 62–3, 70, 87–9, 94
mark-making 14, 29
mental deficiency 18, 24
Ministry of Education 25, 27
murals 57–9

neurological disorder 18, 86
normal children 28–9

obedience 32, 34, 43, 62
oppression 17, 19, 29, 44, 58–9, 63, 76, 81

paraphernalia 59
parents meeting 17–18
'Pass the Ring' game 29, 29 n.12
pedagogy/pedagogical 22, 28, 42, 44, 44 n.18, 61, 82
  liberatory 61
personal identity 13–14
phonetic method 12, 22, 32, 34
photograph/photography 17–18, 87
play/playing 1, 3, 5, 8–10, 14, 23–4, 29–31, 34, 42, 46–8, 54, 58, 61–2, 64, 67, 71, 75–6, 78, 86. *See also* games
poems/poetry 8, 56–7, 57 n.20, 89, 89 n.36, 90
politics/political 3–4, 13, 26, 37, 42–3, 43 n.16, 44, 49–50, 58, 80–93, 81, 83
popular culture 58
primers 2, 4, 7–8, 11, 17, 22, 71, 78, 83, 90–2, 94
psychology 28, 42, 69, 86

quadrilha (square dance) 68, 68 n.25

relaxation 8–9, 23, 33, 76
representation 2, 9, 13–14, 38, 45–6. *See also* self-representation
revaluation 3
rhythms 22, 34, 36, 75
Rocinha, Rio de Janeiro (Brazil) 1, 15, 27, 44, 49, 57, 63, 70, 76, 79, 83, 87, 94
rules, school 10, 32–3

script 2, 7, 12, 16, 24, 60, 70, 89
self-awareness 69

self-representation 13. *See also* representation
self-transformation 33. *See also* transformation
signs 12, 20, 24, 38
  sign-discovery exercises 24, 24 n.11
Skinner-type psychology 28
slave/slavery 62
social class 32
solidarity 93
sound(s) 2, 5, 10, 12, 21–2, 31–2, 34–9, 45–6, 48, 51, 53, 55, 57, 60, 63–5, 67–8, 72, 74, 78, 89–91
Special Education/Special Educational Needs 1, 22, 25–8
Special Students 24–6
storytelling 83
strategic plan 82
strikes 63, 80–2
'Student Performance Record Sheet' 28
student(s) (favela child). *See also* teachers
  with autism 46
  bad 32–3
  dropout 25, 27–9
  with dyslexia 73
  engagement of 69
  family issues 86–7
  individualized work 73, 86
  lack of discipline 33, 34, 47–8, 69
  multi-tasking 73
  teacher-student relations 42, 46, 49, 62–3
  unable to speak 41–2
  violent/troubling 3, 33
study practices 42
syllabic method 12

teachers 5, 10–11, 13, 22, 26–9, 33–4, 41–3, 44 n.18, 46–9, 58, 60–2, 83. *See also* student(s) (favela child)
  first-grade 44, 82
  lay teachers 44
  literacy 2–4, 7, 10, 12, 17, 19, 22, 26–7, 41
  loss of control 48
  strikes 63, 80–2
  teachers' movement 81
  teacher's practice 82
  teacher-student relations 42, 46, 49, 62–3

teaching methods 27, 42
traditional 62
trainee 43
workshops 42
textbooks 15, 33, 41, 59, 71, 91
theatre work in schools 42, 83
theatrical game 11, 61
Tio (older man/uncle) 5, 5 n.1, 14, 60, 91, 94
totalitarianism 28
transformation 4, 73, 81–2. *See also* self-transformation
typewriters 90–1

unconscious minds 10, 13, 19, 33, 43, 67, 82, 88, 92. *See also* conscious/consciousness
Unidade de Ensino (unit of teaching) 82 n.33

Vavá (character) 38, 41, 45, 51, 57, 62, 70, 93
violence 3, 25
institutionalized State violence 77
violent classroom 33, 76–80
'Vivo-Morto, Morto-Vivo' game 23

words 1–3, 7, 16–17, 21, 23–4, 28, 36–40, 40 n.15, 42–3, 45, 49, 51–4, 57, 58 n.21, 63–5, 68 n.26, 69–70, 72 n.27, 75, 77, 87, 89 n.36, 91–2, 94
accents 70
creation of new 3, 38
curse-words 70
generative 13, 13 n.9
mulatto/mulata 57 n.20
word-based literacy (wordification) 12, 26–7
word-building 46
written 1–3, 16, 27, 37

www.ingramcontent.com/pod-product-compliance
Lightning Source LLC
Chambersburg PA
CBHW061845300426
44115CB00013B/2508